AF374505

just say hello

Knock down the walls to discover the ONE relationship that CHANGES EVERYTHING

DARLA CZEROPSKI

FOCUSPOINT Publishing

JUST SAY HELLO: KNOCK DOWN THE WALLS TO DISCOVER THE ONE
RELATIONSHIP THAT CHANGES EVERYTHING
Author: Darla Czeropski, Founder and Visionary of ohsofreeministries.com

This book deals with several sensitive subjects that may trigger your emotions regarding child abuse, sexual assault, physical and emotional abuse, infidelity, substance abuse, and sexual abuse. While the author has taken great lengths to ensure the subject matter is dealt with in a compassionate and respectful manner, it may be troubling for some readers. Discretion is advised.

The content of this book is for informational purposes only and is not intended to diagnose, treat, cure, or prevent any condition or disease.

Understand that this book is not intended as a substitute for consultation with a licensed practitioner. Please consult with your own physician or healthcare specialist regarding the suggestions and recommendations made in this book.

Cover design by *Vanessa Mendozzi* | Cover Photo by *Erin Suchy*

© 2022 Darla Czeropski

This book is protected by copyright laws of the United States of America. This book may not be copied or reprinted for commercial gain or profit. The use of short quotations or occasional page copying for personal or group study is permitted. Permission will be granted upon request.

Scripture quotations marked (NLT) are taken from the Holy Bible, New Living Translation, copyright ©1996, 2004, 2015 by Tyndale House Foundation. Used by permission of Tyndale House Publishers, Carol Stream, Illinois 60188. All rights reserved.

Scripture quotations marked (NIV) are taken from the Holy Bible, New International Version®, NIV®. Copyright © 1973, 1978, 1984, 2011 by Biblica, Inc.™ Used by permission of Zondervan. All rights reserved worldwide. www.zondervan.com The "NIV" and "New International Version" are trademarks registered in the United States Patent and Trademark Office by Biblica, Inc.™

Scripture quotations are from the *ESV® Bible (The Holy Bible, English Standard Version®)*, Copyright © 2001 by Crossway, a publishing ministry of Good News Publishers. Used by permission. All rights reserved."

Scripture quotations marked MSG are taken from THE MESSAGE, copyright © 1993, 2002, 2018 by Eugene H. Peterson. Used by permission of NavPress, represented by Tyndale House Publishers. All rights reserved.

ISBN paperback: 979-8-9853341-0-4 | ISBN Ebook: 979-8-9853341-1-1

All rights reserved.
No part of this publication may be reproduced, stored, or transmitted in any form or by any means – electronic, mechanical, digital, photocopy, recording, or any other – except for brief quotations in printed reviews, without the prior permission of the author or publisher at ohsofree@protonmail.com.

To my husband, Paul. I'm thankful you were the one who reminded me to "just be me." You always make me feel that I'm enough. I'm so grateful God brought you into my life and I'm walking this journey with you.

To my six: Jenny, Evan, Andy, Nathan, Deianna, and Caleb, and the ones they love. Thank you for offering me grace when I wasn't at my best. You've captured my heart.
I love you!

To Brenda, my sister and best friend. You've been beside me through laughter and tears. Thank you for the first edit.

To Rodney, my brother, who read all my childhood stories and told me they were good, even if they weren't.

To Kristi, my bestie since high school. Thank you for cheering me on from a distance.

Thank you to Chester and Virginia Turner,
the best parents in the world!
I know you are beaming in heaven over this accomplishment.
Not because my name is on the cover, but because
I'm becoming more like Jesus every day.

Most of all to my ONE and only, Jesus Christ,
who knocked down my walls, walked me through the rubble,
and has brought me into a loving,
intimate relationship with Him. I want to be more like you.

CONTENTS

From the Bottom of My Heart

This book is special. Not because of me but because of seven beautiful women who divinely stepped into my world. Over the last year, they've shared their life stories with me at coffee shops, kitchen tables, and on my couch with tears, courage, integrity, and grace. They are the Mary's, Esther's, and Rahab's of today, living out their calling to share their stories. They've fought their way through their own wilderness struggles and found the transforming power of God.

Melissa: I'm so thankful I was there when you chose God as your Savior. Thank you for allowing me to dunk you under the water, baptizing you was a first for both of us and an honor. I'm looking forward to seeing what God does through you as you share Jesus with the people of Canada.

Kate: You are a joy! Just being in your presence is like a breath of fresh air. We all exhale when we're around you. Thank you for being on the cover and opening your heart like a book to share God's love with all our readers.

Brandii: Girl, your friendship, mentoring and love have meant more to me than I can express in words. Thank you for being brave and bringing all the darkness in your past into the light on these pages. We both know God brought you into my life for a purpose. My brain thanks you too. Love you!

Samantha: Though we only live thirty minutes apart, God brought us together online through our writer's critique group. He knew I'd need a website designer even before I knew it myself. Your story may not be one of trauma but one we all need to hear and live by. I'm excited you're part of this journey and have become a dear friend.

Megan: Neighbor, it's no coincidence we met. Thank you for saying, "yes" without hesitation. You jumped in the mix at the perfect time. Your smile lights up the room and your faithfulness to always "show up" when needed doesn't go unnoticed.

Tessa: Where you are now isn't the end of the story. God has great things in store for you. Keep the faith, fight the fight, and know God isn't finished yet. I'll always be here believing in you, cheering you on and waiting for God to reveal the moment you walk outside the concrete walls.

Natalie: You stepped in as a gift from God. Thank you for sharing your love story, going above and beyond in this process, and helping to fill an empty space in my heart. Love, your Aunt Darla.

From the Author

My life reflects God's infinite grace. I've discovered through Christ the *me* that He created, not the one changed by this world. I'm an author, wife, mom, friend, and disciple of Jesus. I've experienced a peace only He can provide and I'm excited about the future He's planned for me.

My relationship with God is intimate. My calling is clear. Unfortunately, my past was different than it is now.

I was 18 when I married. The white picket fence I dreamed about quickly turned into a nightmare. I spent years crying in the shower over stressful episodes that sent me spinning out of control. My marriage was filled with negative words spewed in anger, slamming doors, and blaming each other for unmet expectations.

Eventually, I realized I couldn't fix it and felt I'd never be enough. I made hurtful choices I wished I could take back. The circumstances leading to my divorce were devastating. I often plummeted into a pit of past failures. Now, I look back for a different reason: not to sit in my shame or rot in my regret, but to share a story of hope. The journey has been a long one, not perfect, but transformed.

Today, I'm married to a wonderful, godly man and spend my time leading two organizations for Christ. In one, I travel to churches and lead workshops that give women who've experienced trauma an opportunity to form an intimate relationship with Jesus. The second ministry is online and offers women community, hope and vision for their future. The book sessions provide encouragement for them to discover the path they were created for and opportunity to move toward the life He has in store for them.

I'm so excited to share what I've learned, so you can also experience the life God created for YOU!

The God you've wondered

about your entire life

is waiting

on the other side of the wall

Just Say Hello

INTRODUCTION

The door opens and your senses are flooded with calm, comfort, and connection. Breathing in the aroma of coffee beans floating through the air eases your anxiety, a much welcome fix to your increasingly stressful day.

You order your favorite latte while scanning the room to find the perfect table. Between the whirring sound of the coffee machine and the humming voices around the room, familiar tunes find their way to you. Everything is perfect, right?

Not exactly. Life will never be perfect. But for now, meeting with a friend as you laugh about completing each other's sentences makes this world tolerable. This perfectly imperfect relationship is a trusted one. This friendship allows you to be yourself.

I wish this is how a relationship could be between you and me. Instead, you will most likely only know me from within the pages of this book.

Still, I'm hoping the title invited you to open the cover and your heart as well. Your curiosity got the best of you after reading the first sentence. There is a slight shift to your perspective. You've known for a while now you're ready to meet the ONE relationship you've been waiting for your entire life!

Have you ever thought of God in this way? Maybe your thoughts about God have more to do with church or organized religion. Maybe you say you believe in God, but still feel there is something missing. Maybe just the thought of God makes you feel uneasy. It's okay—God gets it! He knows why you hesitate. Timing is important and His timing is perfect.

He has selected a moment for you to meet Him. I believe He began weaving Himself into your thoughts and experiences long before today. Be honest. He keeps bumping into you in the most unexpected moments, right? Sometimes He is just a passing thought. Sometimes a friend brings Him up in conversation. Sometimes you've called out to Him in desperation.

Skeptical? Questions? It's okay. Feeling this way about God is common. I've believed in God for over fifty-nine years but was not serious about following Him. I didn't understand the difference between believing there was a God and having an intimate relationship with Him. I also struggled with walls I'd built to protect myself from being emotionally hurt.

I wrote this book to show you how to identify and knock down the walls you built from experiencing trauma in your life. Through stories from myself and my dear friends you will see you are not alone. My hope is for you to draw close to God and develop an intimate relationship with Him. You start the same way you would when befriending someone. So, here we go; first things first—*Just Say Hello.*

Meeting someone

for the first time is like

opening the cover of a new book;

but with *God* you *begin*

a new chapter of

a never-ending *story*.

CHAPTER 1

EVERY RELATIONSHIP BEGINS WITH HELLO

If you had lived in the 1800s and were one of the first 50 to own a District Telephone Company of New Haven phone book, you would have been instructed to begin your telephone conversation with a firm and cheery 'hulloa'.[1]

Over time, this misheard word of greeting transformed into hello. This is one powerful word! We say this word often when we introduce ourselves and greet others. This small word may seem trivial but carries with it an emotional offering of acceptance.

Human beings are created with an innate desire for relationships but not just any relationship. We long for strong and lasting ones. Most of us first experience how to form relationships by observing our parents.

You're one of two kinds of kids. The child clinging tightly to your mom's hand or the one she chases breathlessly through the crowd. The child who complains of a tummy ache when meeting new people or the no fear type of girl who dances and sings with your dress pulled up over your head. These two types of children act differently when meeting someone new. A stranger says "hello". You either grin so big you can't see your eyes or like me, maneuvered quickly behind your mother's legs to act as a shield. If you are the latter, your parent probably tried to insist you respond, right? Then, it happened. You became a wet noodle collapsing to the floor.

"Oh, they're just shy," mom would remark as you buried your red-blushed cheeks deep within the safety of her lap. Maybe you were shy or maybe not.

Funny thing is, regardless of your personality type, you eventually learned the art of greeting others. The point. Regardless of personality, introductions stir up all kinds of emotions and can be riddled with ups and downs. Why? Expectations.

One of my biggest obstacles in saying hello to new acquaintances is my expectations. I go through scenarios in my mind and wonder if the one I'm meeting will lack interest in me.

I probably have made a mess of some relationships because of my expectations. If they failed, it was because of my unrealistic optimism of how the other person should or shouldn't respond to me.

Do you remember the first time you became interested in boys? I was 13. There were several I wanted to notice me. Among the chatter of hundreds of middle schoolers, I would notice the one I had a crush on. When he'd join our circle, if I was lucky, I would get elbowed and a "hey". This was more like a big brother gesture and my heart would sink into a pool of rejection.

Why? Because I hoped the person would feel the same way I felt about them. Inevitably, my feelings were dashed with disappointment. What I expected was usually a fantasy I had concocted. You know. Boy meets girl and then marriage. Okay, maybe not that drastic.

Thank goodness I made it through those middle school years and hope rose from the ashes of my insecurities. Guess what? I tried "hello" again and again until someone showed interest in me for more than just a buddy. And this wasn't just with the opposite sex. Girl cliches were cruel.

Problem? The more times I was rejected, the more mistrust grew. The bottom line, rejection hurts. However, without being rejected we never realize which relationships are worth our investment.

The quicker we accept rejection as part
of life and use it as a tool to grow,
the quicker we learn rejection can be a blessing.

During the rejection process we often build up walls. These emotional walls we erect are intended to protect our hearts from being broken the next time around. Somewhere down the path, strongholds keep us from experiencing the strongest of all emotions – love. Not just any love. The real deal. Perfect love.

So, what are strongholds? Walls that keep you from cultivating your relationship with God. The simplest way to understand the meaning of stronghold is to think about what has a "strong-hold" on you. You want to be free, but most often you get stuck in the struggle.

You realize you can't go through the wall, so you resort to turning back to old patterns or settling in right next to the wall; this feels comfortable. For this reason, you may also find it difficult to step nearer to God. The best way to break these strongholds in your life is to understand one fact:

God will knock down the walls when you
decide you are ready to step out of the way.

But first, you must ask Him to be in relationship with you. Maybe you're thinking, "I already know God" and wonder if you picked this book up by mistake. My answer to you is, "Probably, not."

I too believed in God but something was missing. I learned "about" God as a child from attending Sunday School at church. I often talked to God, memorized several verses, and loved Youth Night as a teenager. Even as an adult I attended services three times a week. Yet, all of this was not enough. *God wants more.*

He knows you are far from perfect. We all are somewhat rough around the edges. He also knows you feel you will never be good enough; never quite measure up. So, why would He want to be in a relationship with someone like you? Simple. He created you. He only creates what He loves. When you think about it, *God has always had a relationship with YOU!* He is your Creator. This debunks the feeling you could ever be rejected when you say "Hello, God." How could someone who loved you enough to create you, reject you?

From the beginning in the book of Genesis, we see the first glimpse of God's relationship with creation. These historical-based documents found in the Bible have survived thousands of years and remain powerful throughout the scrutiny of man's lifespan. *Most importantly*, the Bible reveals *the heart of God*. The Bible is God's thoughts shared with man in written form.

Trust me. Scripture included in this book is not meant to preach at you. I believe as we study relationships in God's Word, you will understand more fully His entire plan for your life. So here we go! Let's look where God first created relationships. Let's go to the beginning.

I'm not sure how God the Father, Jesus the Word, and the Holy Spirit first got together as one, but I'm guessing since they are ONE, they didn't have to do introductions. You may have heard of the word trinity. For those who haven't, let me explain.

God is one God made up of three different persons. He created us as a triune creature like Himself. We have a spirit, soul, and we live in a body.

We see this more clearly when God says, "Let US make human beings in OUR image, make them reflecting our nature" (Genesis 1:26 MSG).

Wow! Just imagine. God the Father created us in His image and instilled His very nature within us! This scripture reveals how the trinity worked together in the creation process and everything was made by and through them. Who could do a better job working together than these three? What teamwork! Just picture this.

God the Creator sitting at the drafting board, Jesus the faithful and loving Son peering over His shoulder and the Spirit powerfully hovering nearby in anticipation as God begins to unfold His miraculous world.

Then God reveals His most spectacular part of the plan. He creates a living and breathing man out of the dust of the earth. This is where we can see the importance of relationships. This is where we see God has feelings for mankind.

At this moment, God revealed big-time empathy. Empathy is the ability to understand and share the feelings of another. In this case,

God loved Adam so much, He didn't want him to feel lonely. God empathized with the one He created.

He chose to make Adam the perfect someone to share in his journey and to be his companion. Like a beautiful gift wrapped up in perfection, like a father giving his precious daughter's hand in marriage, God presents Eve to Adam. What a wonderful display of love!

There we see it. Adam coming out of a deep sleep, feeling as if he had only taken a long nap. He rubs his eyes and stretches his long limbs to wake up his extremities. Across the way, God, Jesus, and the Spirit are hanging out waiting to present their big surprise. As they see Adam stirring, Jesus and the Holy Spirit elbow each other. A smile lifts from one side of God's face. You can see in their eyes the anticipation of Adam's reaction.

"Woo-hoo! At last!" Adam exclaimed, "This one is bone from my bone, and flesh from my flesh!" (Genesis 2:23 NLT).

Okay. "Woo-hoo" was my interjection. However, from the exclamation marks in the text, we know Adam was ecstatic. There they all were. The Father, the Son, the Spirit, and their greatest creation - Adam and Eve, everyone enjoying each other's company. Do you see what I am seeing? This is God's first example to us of being in a relationship with His creation.

This is God's plan for everyone! From the beginning, YOU were part of His plan and He is waiting for the moment you choose Him.

See how very much our Father loves us,
for He calls us His children, and that is what we are.
1 John 3:1 NLT

God created you in His image. This is important because just as you received attributes from your earthly parents, God gave you characteristics from His image, too. He designed everything about you. He planned your days before you ever breathed and watched every cell of your body form inside your mother's womb.

Job, another man written about in the Bible, lived sometime after 1650 BC and before 1500 BC. God considered him a very righteous (upstanding) man. Job understood God was the Creator. He said, "You guided my conception and formed me in the womb" (Job 10:10).

So, you may ask yourself, "Why would He want to create me?" This is mind-blowing, right? There are millions of ways to design a human and He decided He wanted to create you! It's because you are uniquely different. We know this because scientists have identified the *genetic code*. The human genome alone is made up of about 3 billion chemical pairs and within the genetic code we are 99.9% the same. However, the arrangement of your DNA within the code is different from everyone else's unless you are an identical twin.

During the developmental process, twins demonstrate different likes and dislikes making them unique. They truly have minds of their own. It is because of this uniqueness God wants to have a relationship with you. He made you for His pleasure. He is your Creator and longs to enjoy you because of your unique characteristics. He also created you with the ability to choose Him or not.

Many people believe there is a Creator but never quite grasp God's deepest desire is for relationship. I'm unsure how you feel about God or what you are even thinking as you are reading this. However, I hope you will feel more confident about starting a relationship with God, knowing He already started one with you before you were even created. Here is one example from the Bible which speaks to all human beings about creation.

The Gospel of John reveals that Jesus was with God in the beginning and **everything was made through him** (John 1:1-3 NLT paraphrased). Notice the word, *everything* was made through Jesus. Remember the verse we read above in Genesis 1:26? The one that says, "Then God said, "Let us make human beings in our image, to be like us." Jesus is the *Son*. He was there at the beginning with God and the Spirit and "everything was made through Him." Yes, this includes you.

Just think. Your God took one moment in time to think about who you would be. In love and admiration, He formed you perfectly and has been anticipating the moment you would notice Him since before your conception. God designed the entire you in His perfect, creative mind. He contemplated every intricate detail of you with great precision before ever placing you inside your mother's womb.

> *You (God) made all the delicate, inner parts of my body*
> *and knit me together in my mother's womb.*
> **Psalm 139:13**

Are you unsure "if" God is real? This is where you must have faith. You only need a little faith to experience a powerful love beyond what any human can fathom. If you have never experienced God's love maybe you've unintentionally placed a lock on your heart. However, I have some good news for you! Each lock has a key! In some cases the key is not easily accessible because it has been missing for so long. This makes finding the key a challenge because you are not sure where to start looking. Let me explain.

Have you ever lost your keys? Your heart starts to race and your adrenalin is pumping. You are frantically moving from room to room and anxiously tracing step after step in your memory bank. If you're a woman you're checking your purse and digging deep inside every pocket, becoming more frustrated by the minute! In desperation you dump everything from your bag onto the bed and unzip all the compartments. When it is not found, you check again. Your mind reels with devastating consequences that may occur if your keys are misplaced forever. The outcome doesn't look promising.

The point? If your heart is locked you will need to dig deep, identify what's blocking your progress, and eliminate any reasons for not trusting God. Maybe you keep God stuffed deep within a pocket filled with doubt, disappointment, or fear.

You may ask yourself, "Why would He want a relationship with me when I haven't reciprocated?" Well, the best way I can explain this is quite simple. So simple, people often can't accept it. Here it goes...**God is LOVE!**

I know, right? So, simple. Look at it this way. God is love and creates everything through the law of love.

Why would He create you, knowing you would continually choose so many things to love more than Him? The answer? God is love! Yes, He knew every good and bad choice you would make and every doubtful thought you would ever have; even the ones you're currently processing. He knew all this and created you anyway.

*Nothing you have done and nothing you
do in the future kept God
from breathing life into your lungs.*

This is humbling. Everything you've done and will do in the future has been seen by God. The good and the not-so-good. This means God is omniscient. Nothing takes Him by surprise. He knew everything concerning you even before you entered your mom's womb. Hold on to this point. *He created you regardless!*

Take a big breath. Exhale. Allow this thought to enter the very depths of your soul; the place where you instinctively feel when something is right. Let it melt deep into the part of you God designed for personal moments such as this. HE WANTS YOU! This is His plan. Up to this point, it has mostly, if not completely been a one-sided relationship.

Maybe you believe there is some sort of creator. Maybe you have prayed a few prayers. You may have been to church on Christmas, Easter or attend regularly but still don't feel connected to God.

Having a relationship with someone is more than just waving at an acquaintance across the room. Healthy relationships are ones where we let down our defenses and choose to give everything to the one you want to be in a relationship with. It's work. As most of us know by now, worthwhile relationships take time and effort. *The more you show up; the more you will experience God.*

When you actively include Him in your daily decision-making process and spend time reading about Him in His Word (Bible), you will see His unlimited power working in your life.

History proves to you and me how God works in the lives of those who love Him. His love is so life-changing, people have given up everything just to serve Him. You can find many detailed stories in the Bible of people who chose to obey God like Paul, Peter, and James. These and many others served Jesus and gave their lives for Him.

History books reveal how people like Joan of Arc and Martin Luther served God. Missionaries such as Dr. David Livingstone, Mary Slessor, and Jim Elliot gave their lives to spread the news of Jesus around the world. There is absolutely something to this. For these men and women, believing in God was a choice. Living out their belief was a choice, too.

I want to introduce you to Melissa. She knew very little about God. Yet, when the moment was just right, everything fell into place for her to meet Him. Settle in, refill your cup of coffee, or as Melissa calls it, "double-double" and get comfy as she shares her story.

Melissa

I never imagined attending a neighborhood Halloween party dressed as a witch would start a chain of events that changed my life forever! Nothing was a God-moment in my life. I just didn't think that way. Everything was just a coincidence. I didn't realize God had been working over the past few months to place me and my family in a suburban neighborhood in Oklahoma. It never crossed my mind sitting next to someone also dressed as a witch was part of His plan. Yet, that is exactly what happened. At just the right time in just the right place, God began to reveal Himself to me.

My first thoughts of God were shaped by tradition. When I was six-year-old, my father served at a military base in Canada. My parents would take my siblings and me to Catholic church on the base. I loved going. Though not to learn about God. I didn't even understand what was going on in the Masses. The highlight? Donuts, juice, and hanging out with friends after service.

I moved with my family to another city at the age of fifteen. I'm not sure about the circumstances or why we never re-established going to church. God was mostly non-existent in my mind.

Adult conversations about God leaned towards atheism. He doesn't exist. The Bible is just one story after another that man has concocted. Yet during personal struggles, I would privately ask God, "Why have you forgotten me? Why am I sad? If you are real come and get me out of this." Of course, He never answered. At least not then.

I remember the day my husband, son, and I arrived in Oklahoma from Canada to serve the next four years through the military exchange program. After days of looking for a house, we were exhausted and frustrated. We decided to visit the military base and see if there were any other options. Fifteen minutes before arriving at the squadron office, a house became available. Coincidence? I thought so at the time. Within the hour, the home was rented to us. Just in time to attend the neighborhood annual Halloween party.

I found myself sitting outside around a warm fire introducing myself to Darla and her family. I told them all about how we arrived in Oklahoma. "My husband is in the Canadian Air Force. We will be living in the neighborhood for approximately four years." During the conversation, I mentioned I wanted to meet some ladies. Darla invited me to a new book study in her home the following week.

I ordered the book for the study, *What Happens When Women Say Yes to God*. My husband realized it was a Christian book and couldn't understand why I would go to a study when I didn't even believe in God. "I just want to meet some friends," I replied, dismissing his comments.

I arrived at Darla's home the following week and met three ladies who would become my closest friends for the next four years. As we went around the room introducing ourselves, I felt lost and confused. Then it was my turn.

I said, "I'm not like you guys." Their eyes were filled with questions. Darla asked me what I meant. "Well, I don't believe like you do. I may be an Atheist, Agnostic, or Creationist."

Darla explained this group would be focusing on Jesus and she wanted me to feel welcome. She wanted to get to know me and wanted to know if this was okay with me. She also said even if I didn't want to continue in the group, she still wanted to be my friend.

"I want to stay," I told her. Something I couldn't explain drew me to these ladies. Something just felt right.

Each week we would comb through the pages of the book, filled with inspirational stories of others whose lives were transformed after meeting God. Darla quickly realized I didn't have a Bible. One afternoon she dropped a pink, easy-to-read version of the Bible at my home along with a topical guide which allowed me to find scriptures based on how I was feeling at any given moment. God spoke to my heart as I read His Word. I read it every night and felt God's presence as He spoke to me through the Scriptures.

I felt the presence of God in our time together, a peaceful feeling I couldn't explain. I also observed how God was working in the lives of the ladies who befriended me. As we walked through the pages of Lysa TerKeurst's book and began studying Chapter 3, I knew I wanted to say "yes" to God. I had underlined these words and began to share with the group what they meant to me.

"There is a place I escape to that allows my soul to breathe and rest and reflect. It is the place where I can drop the "yuck" the world hands me and trade it in for the fullness of God. It is a space where God reassures me, confirms that He has everything under control, and gives me a new filter through which I can process life. The Bible calls it the remaining place. I call it my sweet, secret place."[2]

Lysa then pointed us to a scripture where Jesus says, "Remain in me, and I will remain in you. No branch can bear fruit by itself; it must remain in the vine. Neither can you bear fruit unless you remain in me" (John 15:4).

As the conversation turned and I shared what I'd been experiencing over the past few weeks, Darla stopped the study midstream and remarked, "It sounds like you want to ask Jesus to be a part of your life."

Right there in the living room, tears filling buckets, I prayed, "God, I want you in my life." An overwhelming peace flooded my being. I experienced an unfamiliar joy. Just now, recalling the events of that day, I feel God's presence from head to toe.

A year later, I decided to be a part of a church near my home. Not long after, I was baptized. And guess what? I asked Darla to assist me in the baptism. My first water baptism; her first experience baptizing someone. I was so nervous. As I rose out of the water in my red "Made-New" t-shirt, cheers filled the room and I was overjoyed to follow in Jesus' footsteps.

My relationship with God is phenomenal to me. My mornings begin with a simple "hello" to my friend. I worship Him by listening to Christian music in my car, including Him in all my decision-making, and thanking Him for the blessings in my life. Even simple smiles from strangers or the beauty of creation are reminders of God's power in my life. He has become my Father and my Comforter. Living without Him is non-negotiable.

When I recall my story, I realize how God miraculously directed my move from Canada to Oklahoma. Not just to meet new people, but to meet Him. I no longer feel forgotten and the prayer to "come and get me" was answered. All I had to do was say, "Hello, God."

• • •

Every person has their story and timing in how they meet God. Melissa was on God's heart from day one. When the time was right, Melissa accepted His invitation. Maybe you know little about God, yet wonder if He is thinking about you. I can guarantee, **you** are always on His mind. Regardless of our knowledge of God, we must decide to have relationship with Him or not.

Now, let's look at a man in the Bible who was raised knowing God. At the end of David's life, God called him, "a man after his own heart" (1 Samuel 13:14).

King David had a deep relationship with God. Throughout his childhood, he was willing to open his heart to Him and not hold back from Him. He sang to God, wrote poetry to God, and even as a young boy stepped up to do mighty things for God. Did he live a perfect life without mistakes? Absolutely not! He murdered a man. What? Really? Why? Because he wanted the man's wife.

Doesn't sound like he had a very strong relationship with God, does it? Then how is it that God called David, "a man after his own heart," before David died. That's right. God made this honorable, grace-filled statement about David even after he used his power as king to end a man's life. Well, not directly after. David had many conversations with God before he passed away. You can read his humbling words asking God to restore their relationship in the Book of Psalms. In turn, God forgave David and did not hold his sin against Him (Psalm 32).

David understood God knew every thought he had, where he would go every day, when he would rise, and when he would sleep. He understood God knew his past and his future. David knew all this and still sinned big time. He now experienced God's all-forgiving and infinite love.

God is waiting for the moment you also take a few steps closer to meet Him. He knew it would take a while for you to be ready. However, He is patient. King David and Melissa both traded the relationship with Him for counterfeit loves and affections. He knows you will do this repeatedly. Yet, when they called out and humbly presented their life to Him, He began to make Himself known to them.

He will do the same with you. He waits. Waits for you to take a step toward Him. Waits for you to be somewhat vulnerable. Waits for you to walk across the room and say, "Hello, God. It's me. Sorry it took so long!"

You may hear hurtful and

harmful voices in your mind.

Turn your thoughts to God

He will extinguish the darts

of condemnation

soaring in your direction.

CHAPTER 2

VULNERABLE CONVERSATIONS

The discussion at a family gathering revolves around everyone's occupations. Feeling that your job is subpar to other family members in your age group, you excuse yourself for another piece of dessert. No one would guess you feel you don't measure up.

Or, you have plans to meet someone for coffee. You struggle with what to wear and worry about what to talk about. Anxiously, you decide to text and say you won't be able to make it.

These two scenarios require you to put yourself out there and be emotionally invested. This means you must be vulnerable. Emotional vulnerability occurs when you are willing to acknowledge your emotions, especially in difficult or painful situations. It's important to be vulnerable in long-lasting relationships because we invest by sharing our deepest emotions.

This is also applicable in our spiritual relationship with God. Author Mark W. Baker, in an article by Relevantmagazine.com, wrote, "We were created for connection to God and others; vulnerability is the requirement for achieving that purpose."[3] So how do we achieve vulnerability with God?

For most people this happens through prayer and studying His word. I find my relationship with God is deeper and more authentic depending on the amount of time I spend with Him. My prayers, which sound more like vulnerable chats, have allowed me to become closer in our relationship. The more I share, the more I feel His presence.

For you these conversations may seem one-sided. You ask a lot of questions while He listens. You unload on God everything He already knows about you and He accepts you as you are. However, just because you don't hear an audible voice doesn't mean He is not answering.

God created you and has been patiently waiting for you to develop a relationship with Him. Your patience is also needed in this process. The longer you have a relationship with God, the more you can pick up on His cues or internal promptings, see lines in His Word pop out from the page, and even recognize when He sends others to share godly wisdom and encourage you.

Relationships take time. Relationships take trust. It takes choosing to do your part. When you think about it, God has had a relationship with you since before you were born. I think He has made it clear that He isn't going anywhere. Now, it's up to you.

> *Vulnerability is one of the first steps in*
> *building a lasting relationship.*

Maybe your story is quite sensitive. Maybe you're afraid to open your heart and life to God because if you do things won't work out. Are you afraid you will have to give up parts of your life to be in a relationship with God? Being vulnerable can be scary!

This is where trust and truth are important. For any relationship to be strong and withstand the test of time you must be forthcoming with any weaknesses that may hinder the relationship. You must share your thoughts, feelings, and challenges. This is how true intimacy is achieved. This is how we ultimately feel accepted and loved. We all want this….do we not?

Author Tracie Miles, in an article entitled "Get Real" stated, "In today's society, we tend to focus more on outward appearances than on the inward condition of our hearts. We may have a smile on our face on the outside; but on the inside, our heart is aching, and our soul is pleading for someone to care enough about us to speak with God on our behalf...we must be willing to expose our weaknesses, shed our hypocrisy and stop pretending our life is a bowl of cherries.

God calls us to be transparent."[4]

We must remove walls the world has used to restrict us and allow God's transformation process to begin.

I've hidden parts of my story many times throughout my life while working to build relationships with people. I was guarded with the information I shared and covered up my insecurities, weaknesses, and fears within the relationships I invested in. This doesn't mean we should tell everything to everyone. However, in our deepest relationships like marriage, vulnerability is a must. In the process of concealing my struggles, I didn't realize how detrimentally this could affect my emotions and physical well-being.

Now, I understand God allows us to share every part of our story with Him. He wants to encourage and heal our hearts and minds. Jesus stated, "For everything that is hidden will eventually be brought into the open and every secret will be brought to light" Mark 4:22 (NLT). We can't hide anything from God. God wants to use every detail about our lives; even things causing us hurt and shame.

He takes our struggles and uses them in ways we can never imagine to fulfill our longings and bring us joy!

We should be mindful when we share our stories to use wisdom. I'm not encouraging you to blast all your sins to the world. We need to be careful to whom we offer vulnerable information. Some personal details should only be shared with a licensed professional whom you know will keep their oath of privacy as you walk through the healing process.

However, there is one with whom you can share everything. God already knows your struggles. Allowing Him to lift the burden of negative past experiences will bring freedom and peace to your life. He takes your shame, restores your life, and redirects your story to His purpose.

When hurts are hidden, they cannot be healed. We are not being truthful with God or ourselves when we hide behind the mask of our sin. As they say, sin thrives in secrecy and denial.

It took me a long time to "own" my story. I was steeped in guilt and shame. I still struggle with my past from time-to-time and find it difficult to forgive myself for hurting the people in those relationships. Dwelling on my past failings keeps me swimming in a gulf of pain. I try to embrace the Apostle Paul's words, "Forgetting what is behind and pressing forward…" (Philippians 3:13 NIV); words reminding me that God doesn't want me to wade in unforgiveness.

I still struggle. Why? Because I often feel I deserve all the pain I have caused others. I tell myself, *everyone who knows my story stands with their jaw dropped staring at the subject matter of my sin.* I wrestle with my guilt, condemnation, pain, fear, anger, and disappointment. My mind tells me, "God has forgiven me," but pride says, "it's not enough, I have to pay for what I did." Will I ever forgive myself? Will I ever accept God's love is enough?

Through many conversations with God, I begin to believe the truth that God loves me even though I've sinned. God has taught me He never looks at me the way I see myself or even the way others see me. God sees what He created and what I will become.

This is how He sees you too! For a long time, I struggled with the girl who said she loved God but looked far different from what she claimed to be. I went to church three times a week, recited numerous scriptures, sang in the choir, played piano for services, and even was on the staff of the preschool at the church where I grew up. Sounds religious, right?

There I was, an adult with an upside-down life. I was confused about my relationship with God and crushed because I couldn't see, hear, or feel Him working in my day-to-day messiness. Desperate to make sense of who I was, I watched my life spiral out of control. Did I even believe in God? If so, did He still care about me? God revealed Himself to me within my struggle and used the mess to reveal *my need for Him.* I realized I couldn't "fix" everything or "please" everyone.

It's been a long journey. I'm still working on many of these areas.

What I'm about to share still makes me nervous and still evokes some pain and anxiety. I worry people will think differently of me when they read the truth. Yet, I'm hopeful in sharing my story, you'll find the freedom to let go of *your* past failings and live out what God has called you to be.

Darla

Dwelling on the past is never good. Painful memories cause feelings of self-condemnation and chronic unworthiness. Thinking too deeply about the circumstances leading to my divorce is devastating. I quickly plummet into the pit of past failures. A pit I dug for myself.

Recalling the events surrounding my story causes my chest to tighten as if my lungs are in a vice. However, I look back for a different reason: not to sit in my shame or rot in my regret, but to share a story of hope. You will see as you glimpse inside my heart a journey of hurt, hope, healing, and headway.

» HURT

At the age of 41 with two small children, I stood in an Oklahoma court room before the judge after twenty-three years of marriage. From behind the towering bench came words I could hear, but barely process. The judge asked me was I sure I wanted to dissolve my marriage. "Really?" I thought. "No, I'm not sure!" Like an out-of-body experience, I didn't feel alive and wondered if I would pass out. I wanted to run and wished someone had been there to say, "It's okay, RUN!"

Maybe, if someone had been there and could have promised everything would be better, I would have kept on trying. Yet, I was alone.

The documents said we were "incompatible." I was only eighteen years old when we tied the knot and a multitude of obstacles worked against us, immaturity being at the top of the list. I didn't consider the numerous times I saw the flashing caution lights before marrying.

Instead, I sailed through life oblivious to the dangers ahead.

We lived on a rollercoaster of drama. I was frustrated because I didn't get my way. He would try to convince me I was wrong. We argued about everything. This was the cycle. Sadly, we didn't have the skills to communicate and resolve conflict.

After years of fighting and two kids later, I was a mental wreck. Too many years of crying in the shower over a multitude of things, spewing negative words we couldn't take back, and blaming each other led to feelings of rejection. I couldn't fix us both and I always felt I would never be enough. He probably felt the same way, too.

Finally, I had enough. I'm not sure when I decided I was getting out of the marriage. Not sure when the thought went from "God help me" to "I will fix this myself." Deep inside my heart the thoughts turned to lies. I started believing I needed out to keep my sanity and protect my children from the constant battle of the wills. I was exhausted at trying to be a buffer and I wanted relief.

The devil and his cohorts were ready and waiting to take me on a detour away from God's plan onto a side road of harmful and prideful choices. One day, a male friend overheard me crying and asked me what was wrong. I began sharing my marital problems. I told him I was unsure how much longer I could live with the pain.

He sympathetically told me he understood and often felt the same way in his marriage. This was the first of many conversations. Conversations leading us onto shaky ground.

Where was God in all of this?
He was there warning and convicting.

He worked behind the scenes to send other godly individuals to inadvertently caution against the choices we would make. God even opened a door for us to escape by giving my friend a new job in another state. I was relieved.

I would like to tell you my marriage took a turn for the better. The arguing continued and my integrity had been frayed around the edges. I was thankful God had given me a way out. A year later, they moved back into town.

I tried to keep my distance even though his wife kept asking us to hang out and confided she thought we didn't want to be friends with them. That's all it took. My people-pleasing personality caved. After months of hanging out as couples everything went awry. We crossed more lines and feared where things were headed. We both knew we had to stop. I ended up going to a counselor to help me get my life back on track. Unfortunately, I went to an unlicensed counselor. He threatened if I didn't tell my husband within 24 hours, he would.

I need to pause here. I'm sure you are shaking your head in disgust if you are a counselor reading this. How unethical, right? If you are someone considering going to a counselor, please take my advice. There is a reason why we have "licensed" counselors. Choose one who will encourage you and offers you trust with your sensitive information as you take steps to heal.

Driving home, I cried so hard the road was hardly visible. I pulled to the side of the road to throw up. From there everything spiraled out of control. I confessed to my husband and he did what most men do…got angry.

I guess you are wondering how far the infidelity went. You're wanting to ask if we had sex. No, we didn't. Sex or not, the mental and physical lines we crossed caused damage. I no longer felt I could attend the church where I grew up. The relationships my husband and I formed through the years ended abruptly. No one was willing to hold our hands and help us navigate through the aftermath because they didn't want to choose sides. This made me feel rejected and forgotten. Yet, I deserved it, right? So, that was that.

I tried to do everything right going forward: be the perfect wife, be the perfect mother, say "yes" to everyone who had a need. People-pleasing was at an all-time high. Tasks that seemed simple before became overwhelming. Going to the grocery store was a struggle. Who would I run into? Who would see me and know what I did? I felt like I was walking around with a big "U" tattooed on my forehead. She's unfaithful! Stay away from her!

My husband and I went to couples' counseling. A licensed one this time. He went just long enough for me to keep from jumping off the nearest bridge. Counseling is only as good as what you put into it. So, when he stopped going, I moved out taking my two children with me.

I gave up trying to be good. I had messed everything up with God, so why did it matter? Life was exhausting. I tried to find a new church but felt uncomfortable under the weight of condemnation I was carrying. Everything was more than I could handle.

I started a new job as a piano and voice teacher in a nearby music studio. I began hanging out with my co-workers after work at bars where they performed. This helped to mitigate my loneliness. I wasn't a drinker, but found alcohol stopped the pain momentarily. I laughed like I hadn't in years. The music helped drown out the negative voices telling me I wasn't good enough. When morning came, the hangover reminded me of my worthlessness.

All the while my husband was keeping an eye on me. This made me feel I was being stalked and only caused me more anxiety. He continued to cause an endless wave of drama; showing up at places without notice. I didn't realize he was grasping to keep our relationship intact. A relationship unrepairable from my perspective.

I did what I thought was the only answer to stop the rollercoaster ride of emotions. I filed for divorce. My mind and body were depleted. All I could do was go through the motions. I never came to the point of taking my life, but did consider scenarios and how they might relieve my constant anxiety. Running away and never looking back circled my thoughts. Then my children's faces would cause me to break down in tears. I knew I needed to try harder to make the changes necessary for a better life.

My prideful choices had brought me to this place. The problems hadn't been fixed; only made worse.

» HOPE

There I was staring at the garage door in the driveway of the house I rented. I was at my lowest point. I missed my relationship with God; walking with Him and talking with Him. I didn't feel worthy to be His child. Guilt and shame weighed heavy on my heart.

One thing I did know. I knew enough from going to church that God would forgive me if I asked. Feeling empty I cried out to God and asked Him to forgive me for how I had acted and the choices I made. I still remember the words I spoke that day.

"If you will begin to turn my life around,
I will not even take a breath without asking you first."

Humbly, I placed my life in His hands. I slept better that night. In the days following, I spent as much time as possible talking to God. I was anxious about my future and knew I needed to allow God to restore my mind, heart, soul, and strength. I immersed myself in worship music and memorized verses which helped me focus and build trust in Him. The more time I spent with God, the more I felt His peace. The more peace I felt, the more I could trust everything was going to be okay. I had reason to hope because my faith told me that even though I couldn't see my future – God was in control.

» HEALING

Forgiving myself was arduous. After 17 years in my new marriage, I still experience the fallout from time to time. I have regrets and even shame which peeks out from dark corners.

God continuously works to
heal and restore my life.

Healing is not just for physical sickness. God heals everything that is broken. He repairs, restores, and completely transforms all areas of our life that we entrust to Him.

I found memorizing Scripture was the most powerful tool in my healing process. The more I spoke His words aloud, the stronger I became. The more I believed I was His child, the braver I walked. The more I acknowledged that He had everything in control, the more peace I felt. It didn't happen overnight, but God used my weaknesses to show how powerful He is.

» HEADWAY

What is headway? The forward movement of progress, especially when circumstances are slow and difficult. That describes my life exactly. In one moment, I think everything is going great. I'm keeping up in the race. The pace picks up and I'm feeling strong. Then, I trip over my shoelaces and tumble headfirst as everyone else runs by. A shadow is cast over me and kind hands help me to my feet. They assist me as I limp to the sidelines and offer me a drink of refreshing water. Exhaustion hits me like a ton of bricks. Worse, I feel disappointed. Thankfully, I didn't break anything; I'm still in one piece.

This is a daily process. Here on this earth, there is a struggle. My mind points out where I fall short. Jesus reminds me that He is ALWAYS with me. My relationship with God is one I cherish. He is my best friend, confidant, is constantly creating new opportunities for me to experience Him. I'm excited about getting to meet Him face to face and experience "...the new things, of hidden things unknown to you" (Isaiah 48:6 NIV), which He has planned for me.

• • •

My journey may pale in comparison to what you have gone through in your life. Regardless of the weighted baggage you've been carrying, healing is possible through an intimate relationship with God. Vulnerability is part of this process. I realize being vulnerable is not a favorite past time for anyone.

This doesn't mean you have to write a book and share your story publicly. Maybe you could start by writing your story in a journal or share your struggle with a trusted friend. I found faith-based counseling is helpful. When you locate the right therapist, their expertise can assist you in finding the best plan of action to help you in the healing process.

Regardless, you should start by laying everything out before God. He is the perfect one to internally share your hurts, frustrations, and weaknesses because He listens with a loving heart. He does not desire to have a relationship with you to condemn you.

The Bible tells us, "God sent his Son (Jesus) into the world NOT to JUDGE the world, but to SAVE the world through him" (John 3:17 NLT). He came to save us from the walls that separate us from His presence. Sin stems from choosing something or someone to love more than Him. He longs for us to experience His love and power that is life-changing and brings peace and joy beyond what we can even imagine.

You will recognize the lies that have kept you from meeting God as you have vulnerable conversations with Him. These lies have formed huge barriers or walls that cause feelings of frustration, anxiety, failure, and shame.

In the next few chapters, we will look at a few of the most common strongholds. Through personal stories from my friends, you will discover how rejection, fear, perfectionism, busyness, and pride can keep you from experiencing a love beyond your imagination.

The Lord will not reject his people;

he will not abandon

his *special possession*.

Psalm 94:14

CHAPTER 3

WALL OF REJECTION

Have you ever tried to encourage someone who is feeling rejected? Maybe they didn't get the job they wanted. Maybe they invested in a relationship that failed. The circumstances leading to rejection are endless. Unfortunately, rejection is part of our life on this earth. When it finds us, there isn't much anyone can do to fix it. It's just a feeling we must journey through until we find someone or something to replace it. Someone will finally say, "I'm here for you, no matter what."

Some rejection can be shaken off like ants on a picnic blanket. Those little creatures may seem irritating, but a quick snap of the blanket and a slight move to another area saves the day. We often handle some rejection in the same way. We dust ourselves off and move to the next item on our list.

Rejection can cause a debilitating effect on our self-esteem long after the actual events have transpired. In many instances, we may begin to believe the negative words being spewed at us. Author and Dr. David Ward wrote, "Remember that a key message that rejection brings is, 'I am unlovable or unworthy.' We can only hear these painful messages for so long before we start to believe that we deserve that rejection, especially if those seeds were planted in our childhood years."[5] Does an infant deserve to be abandoned? What toddler or child deserves to be told they are worthless?

Rejection occurring multiple times in our childhood causes anxiety to increase and coping skills to wear thin as an adult. You often feel you're hanging on the last thread of hope. You lay your head down for a needed, comfy night's sleep and the tape begins to play. Over and over in your head, you consciously envision scenarios from bad past experiences. You don't just see it in your mind; you feel it.

Maybe your parent failed to keep hundreds of promises, your best friend in school humiliated you, your professor wouldn't budge and give you a needed grade to graduate, your fiancé didn't show up for the wedding, or your spouse packed their bags and moved out. Maybe you have experienced emotional or physical abuse, maybe even sexual abuse. You try to believe the individuals in your life care for you, but the pain you experience proves differently. Yes, rejection is painful and isn't experienced just when it occurs. Oh no! Depending on the severity and the fallout, rejection may plague you for the unforeseeable future. A future filled with feelings of anger, sadness, bitterness, anxiety, depression, mistrust, and even despair.

My friend Kate has experienced her fair share of being rejected. Her story is filled with trauma and pain. The trust she gave to those she loved was stomped on and thrown back in her face.

Kate shares her story because she hopes you too will meet the God who destroyed her wall of rejection and continues to transform her life daily.

Kate

My knees hit the floor. I crumbled in a heap like a discarded rag doll – worthless to everyone. Tears of shame violently flowed leaving a puddle beneath me. I wanted to die, but then I remembered the heartbeat: the tiniest sign of life within me. I cried, "God, why me?" My teenage brain resorted to blaming the only One who might be listening. Obviously, I was wrong.

There was nothing but silence.

I grew up in a Christian church although my parents were raised Catholic. They started attending a Christian church near our home when my mom was pregnant with me. Not long after I was born, my dad quit going. That's not all he quit. He was a workaholic and absent for most of my childhood. My mom continued to take me to our church where I learned to be a good little girl. When we would go out to a restaurant everyone would say how well-behaved I was. They didn't see our nice Christian family was far from Christ-like behind closed doors.

By the time I reached thirteen, I had decided no one really cared about me. I rebelled. At fourteen years of age, I started smoking cigarettes and struggled with watching porn on my computer. My mom tried to control me by calling me every expletive she could think of. My dad was physically abusive. This only confirmed my feelings that I was unworthy.

I struggled with getting enough sleep for several years and had horrifying dreams. By the time I turned sixteen, one dream reoccurred every night. I couldn't make sense of what I was seeing: my step-grandpa sexually abusing a small child. It was later confirmed the child was me.

Smoking weed and drinking became a daily pattern to numb the pain. I searched for anything and everything to make me feel I was valued. At seventeen, I met a boy and sex became my "go-to." I thought I would feel loved being this close to someone, but this was not the case. Under the influence of drugs, I began experimenting with same-sex relationships thinking this might be the answer. Again, I was wrong. My mind was a mess and suicidal thoughts crept in as I planned a way to escape. But with each new day, I would find a reason to go on.

I decided to get my first job working at a food establishment, thinking independence was the answer. My boss was eleven years older than me and was dating a friend of mine. He took me under his wing and became the big brother I never had. One night, He asked if I wanted to go over to his house after work and hang out. He gave me some laced weed to smoke and suddenly everything spiraled out of control. I remember kicking, scratching, and trying to get away. Several hours later, I awoke in the parking lot next to my car.

On my eighteenth birthday, my dad kicked me out of the house. Literally two minutes after I turned eighteen, I was homeless. Sleeping on friends' couches became the norm. My old boyfriend was back in the picture. I started popping pills to stop the emotional pain I was experiencing.

Finally, a friend took me in. Their family was Mormon. I was a senior in high school and they gave me a home. They had rules, but the consistency helped me more than I wanted to admit. I was able to homeschool and quit smoking. I tried to be a good girl. One of the rules I agreed to follow was joining their nightly group to pray and read the Book of Mormon. Figuring out what I believed was a struggle at the time because everyone I had loved told me or showed me, I was worthless. In my mind, God felt the same way, too.

I continued sleeping with my boyfriend. Then, the inevitable happened. I got pregnant with his child and desperately thought. "How is this possible, I'm on birth control!" I told him no one else could know. The secret was buried for three months. Guilt pressured me to show the ultrasound pictures to the family I was living with. They were upset. The dad who had been the only father figure to me over the past several months sat me down for a serious conversation and said, "You realize because you have done this, no one will want you. No one will want to marry you." I was devastated.

With no other choice, I moved back home. All my dreams were shattered. I wouldn't be going to nursing school, I wasn't married, and I would be a burden to my parents. To make things worse, every conversation with my boyfriend turned to adoption. I was so confused and unsure of what I wanted. My decision-making processes were non-existent; my brain was a mess.

One day, my boyfriend called and said he needed to talk to me. I was excited thinking he might want to make our relationship permanent. This may be the answer to my problems. I drove to his house and knocked on the door. Through a small crack he said, "I don't love you and never want to see you again." The door slammed shut.

Like a knife stabbing me in my chest, all the air flowed out of me. I don't even remember the drive home. The two hours of crying on my bedroom floor seemed like an eternity. I knew something had to change, but I didn't know how to fix it. I began crying out to God to fill the gaping hole in my heart. I wanted to die and begged God to take me.

In an instant my mind cleared. I remembered the heartbeat, the tiniest sign of life within me. I felt God's arms of love. I knew then everything would change.

I started attending the college group at a church near my home. There I was, big and pregnant, singing worship songs to God. This group of people made me feel more loved than ever before in my life.

One night, I was in my bedroom praying and reading the Bible. I felt God impress on me to dedicate my baby to the Lord. I was unsure of what dedicating meant, but I laid my hands on my belly and said, "Lord, I'm giving him to you." In that moment God gave me the name Luke Israel. Later, I found out Luke means light. God had become the light of my life. I was freed from my suicidal mindset and given a purpose. I would take care of my child because God was taking care of me.

When my baby was born, my boyfriend showed up at the hospital. We began seeing each other off and on, but I wouldn't sleep with him. I prayed and asked God to help me in the relationship. I wanted to do what was right.

One morning, when I was taking a shower and thinking about my life going forward, Jesus spoke, "Kate, you don't need to be with any man, you only need me." I got dressed, went to my boyfriend's house, and ended it. I told him the Lord showed me my worth and I was worth more than this.

Luke Israel was five months old when I was baptized. I stood in front of the church with my story scribbled on a piece of notebook paper. I had invited my family, knowing they wouldn't show up. I included the story where I was sexually abused by my step-grandpa, not realizing my mom was in the congregation. She wasn't aware of the abuse and confided she'd also been abused as a child.

My life is different now, so much different. Sometimes, I can't wrap my head around the transformation God has done in my life. I'm a pastor's wife, who would've thought? I have four beautiful children and love being a mom. I didn't become the nurse I once thought I would be. Instead, I'm a Doula. I assist woman during childbirth and provide support to their family after the baby is born. The joy in helping young women bring new life into this world is indescribable.

I still struggle with trust in relationships. Recalling my past brings heartache as I think about the girl who laid on the floor like a worthless rag doll. But then I'm reminded of who I belong to. Jesus comes rushing in and wraps His loving arms around me. I hear His voice whisper in the depths of my soul. He says, "Tell that girl, 'She only needs me.'"

• • •

Do you see any similarities in Kate's story to your own? Do thoughts about your past invade your mind causing your stomach to tie up in knots? Do you struggle and ask, "God, why did this happen to me?"

The wall of rejection rises higher and higher as our trust is compromised. You've grown into a mature adult woman, yet the wall remains a regular fixture in your life. Maybe you've gone to counseling and still find yourself repeating old patterns. You've dusted yourself off numerous times, placed that big smile on your face, and taken steps forward to build a better life; only for feelings of rejection to slap you in the face again.

Where is God in all this? He's there. He's waiting on the other side of the wall, ready to take it down. He's been there all the time. I'm sure you're wondering why He hasn't done something by now to help you out of this mess. I love this quote by Therapist Shannon Alder.

There will always be someone willing to hurt you,
put you down, gossip about you,
belittle your accomplishments and judge your soul.
It is a fact that we all must face. However, if you realize that
God is a best friend that stands beside you when others cast

stones you will never be afraid,
never feel worthless and never feel alone. [6]

God has principles or rules He set in motion. As you begin to know Him, you will begin to understand some of the reasons God allows rejection. Here is one I'll let you in on.

God is not the God of rejection.

He never intended for His creation to reject those they have responsibility for. But does this happen? Absolutely! God hates rejection, but knows it falls under the category of human choice.

Think about the individuals in your life who have rejected you. You can agree in some cases your life is better off without them because they continue to reject you repeatedly.

Many of us looked back and realized that without the rejection and the subsequent healing and restoration, we would not be who we are today. God wants to take the rejected heart and pour His all-powerful love into the space.

When the process begins the wall begins to crumble. Will there still be challenges? Yes. Many underlying feelings and past experiences must be addressed to remove every stone you have placed around your heart. However, this time you will be in a relationship with the One who knows you best. He knows just what you need. This transformation may take time as God heals your heart, mind, soul, and even physical damage caused by past trauma. Maybe you blame yourself or others. Maybe you blame God.

You are not alone. Freedom can only be established when we allow God to destroy the wall. How does this happen? We must acknowledge God is above all and ask Him to remove it. This is how to begin an intimate relationship with Him.

You may have decided it's much easier to pull up a chair and just deal with the circumstances involving the trauma you have experienced.

You tell yourself, "This is just life, so that is that." The longer we sit by the wall the more we may find ourselves justifying our circumstances and holding on to the past.

God wants to move you toward something new. At first, you may not see what He is doing. You may not trust Him and feel He will treat you the same as everyone you've previously trusted who has let you down. However, when you establish an intimate relationship with God, you will not only believe in Him, you will really know Him. Through this intimate relationship you will begin to see how He is love and everything He allows is filtered through love, even the hard things. But trust is the only way to find the one true love you are searching for. We must be open-minded and open-hearted to experience perfect love.

God created you to walk with Him, talk with Him and ultimately live with Him in heaven, a place of perfect love He is creating just for you. The only requirement He set in motion is to "love God with all your heart, mind, soul and strength and love your neighbor as yourself." Did you get that? Not the part about loving God; that's a given. The part about loving yourself. Yes, God commands us to love ourselves. I know when you are knee-deep in feelings of rejection, the last thing on your mind is loving yourself. But God has made a way for you to accomplish this. He stands in the gap loving you until you are strong enough to love yourself. Picture this:

- » In the dark night on the cold floor, He is watching you.
- » In the fetal position in a puddle of tears, He is waiting for you.
- » When you feel you are unworthy of love, He screams, "You are worthy!"
- » When you feel no one loves you; He loved you first.

You might be thinking, I didn't see Him on the floor, feel Him in the puddle, or hear His voice. There is one more thing you should understand about God. He never pushes Himself on you. He waits in the shadows for you to trust in Him.

Even though you may have experienced evil, hate, lies, and unimaginable hurt, God is working behind the scenes. He's always had a plan. The problem is we keep trying to "fix" our problems and control our destiny by making our own chooses and placing other things before Him.

"Fixing" is like writing our own chapter
with scenes that don't fit in God's plan.

We keep adding more relationships, places, and things to our story without His guidance. We leave Him out of our decision-making process and think we have full control of our life. This is a lie and the wall of rejection remains. But this may not be the only wall that stands in your way. There may be multiple walls blocking your way to freedom. Some walls have other walls attached, just as our feelings can be intertwined. When a person feels rejected, they may also deal with feelings of fear which we will discuss in the next chapter.

Such love has no fear,

because

*perfect love
expels all fear.*

If we are afraid,

it is for fear of punishment,

and this shows that we haven't

*fully experienced
his perfect love.*

1 John 4:18 NLT

CHAPTER 4

WALL OF FEAR

Someone once told me that they "have to" believe in God. They "have to believe or go to hell." I struggled and knew my words would not make any difference. Tears welled up from behind my lashes. I felt sad and I believe God felt sad, too.

Do you live in fear of punishment from God? Do you feel you will never measure up? Do you feel afraid to even approach God because of mistakes you've made? Maybe you feel the lifestyle you are living would never be acceptable to God. God wants you to understand one thing:

> *"I did not send my son, Jesus, into the world to*
> *condemn the world, but to save the world"*
> John 3:17 (paraphrased)

The fear associated with punishment is not a characteristic of God's love. This fear is derived from a distortion of God's truth.

Have you been involved with a religious community steeped in condemnation? Maybe as a child you have experienced fear from parents or other authoritative figures who used abusive tactics to keep you in line and keep you silent. Or, maybe you experience abuse now? Let me remind you—God is the God of love and he hears you.

No matter what lie you have learned that evil forces are using to separate you from God, truth says, "GOD IS THE GOD OF LOVE."

In her book *Hidden Potential*, Wendy Pope states, "Fear meddles in our rational thinking causing us to doubt everything we know about God."[7] Wow! Can you relate? Has fear whispered that you won't measure up, won't be strong enough, or you aren't capable of being good enough for God? Or maybe it has laughed, "Who do you think you are? Look what you have done. Look what you have become." Maybe you doubt because you don't know the truth of what God wants to do in and through your life.

I'd like for you to meet my friend, Brandii. Though there are several miles between us, I felt her pain as she shared a bit of her story in a recent monthly writer's group meeting. She mentioned how condemnation from past religious experiences had caused her to build emotional walls separating her from the one true God of love. I hope as you read her story, you will realize that you are not alone.

Brandii

Anxiety gripped my entire body. I feared I would be struck by lightning and set on fire by entering the doors of a church. I was alone. Maybe this wasn't such a good idea. I could see stranger's heads turn in my direction from the corners of my eyes. "Don't look at them," I thought, "Just keep moving." I sat near the back and took a deep breath. I was still alive. "Just one of many *twisted and warped lies I was taught to make me live a life of fear.*"

If you ask my family and friends to describe me, they would say I was fearless, brave, and bold. The first to take a step and stand out when others won't. Yet, this was not how I described myself, at least not in the beginning.

I am the sixth child born in my family of fourteen children. Like all families we had our share of problems. As a child I thought our family was like every other family. The older I became the secrets of how dysfunctional we were surfaced like weeds in an unkempt garden. Secrets we kept within the walls of our house. Why?

Indiscretions of any kind are frowned upon by the Jehovah's Witnesses. Every detail of one's life is scrutinized, judged, and sentenced. This kept us chained to deceit and mistrust. Our family didn't discuss our problems or work to resolve them. This led to depression, anxiety, and fear that affected each of us.

Before I was born, my parents had serious marital issues impacted by the death of my older brother at the age of three months. My father grieved in silence. Unable to seek outside help for fear of scrutiny from other Jehovah's Witnesses, he turned to other women and alcohol for understanding and comfort. My mother's grief turned to bitterness when my father confessed his indiscretions. My parents weren't the only ones with secrets. Remember, my siblings and I were taught to keep everything hidden. Our closets were stuffed with years of ugliness and pain. What I'm about to share is not just embarrassing but heartbreaking.

I was sixteen when my mother divorced my father. I worried the Elders would punish my family if they knew the truth. I lived in constant fear. In a moment of teenage rage, I cornered my mother and everything spilled out. I told her about the many years I tried to protect my younger sisters and myself from being sexually abused by my older brothers. I never realized they were abusing my younger brothers too.

Naïvely, I thought my mother would make changes in our home and would help protect me and my younger siblings. I was wrong. Although I felt an incredible amount of relief bringing the abuse out in the open, it was short-lived. My mother went into a deep depression. She barely could take care of herself much less her children. I became the caretaker of my siblings.

I can remember allowing my siblings to sleep on my bedroom floor or in my bed to protect them from my older brothers sexually assaulting them. I also worried about other children we associated with because my mom continued to allow my brothers to babysit for other single mothers whom my mom befriended. I would beg her to not allow this. Remember, I was still a child. Her response to my fear and accusations, "there is no proof they are doing this now." There was one single mom of four girls who trusted my mom and had no idea of any problems with my brother sitting for her children. We now know that he raped one of them and molested one of the others. Everything was out in the open. "FINALLY! SOMEONE IS GOING TO STOP THIS," I thought. The allegations were brought to the Elders. They did nothing to speak of. Nothing except tell us to keep those situations "in house." Then there was silence. Those children were never helped and law enforcement was never told about it. This was a common practice within the Jehovah's Witnesses congregation.

I battled in my mind with how everything was handled. How could the Elders allow this? How could God allow this? Answers never came and the habit of silence continued.

At seventeen my mother and older sisters began pressuring me to be baptized. We were taught that young girls must be baptized in order to marry other baptized Jehovah's Witnesses men. Under duress, I did what they expected. I stood before the congregation bawling uncontrollably, wishing there was a way out. I would be expected to marry within the next two years and have children or devote myself to full-time ministry.

I dropped out of high school in the 10th grade. Education is frowned upon with the JW's. Having few skills to offer any prospective employers, I started dating when I was eighteen. There were only two eligible men available in my local congregation. One had been married before and was 11 years older than me. The other was known for having a very angry temper. I chose the first, thinking it was the safer choice. After a 6-month courtship, the Elders required us to be married immediately knowing we were acting promiscuously.

At the age of nineteen, after three months of marriage, I became pregnant. I knew nothing about parenting but I was sure my child would not be physically or sexually abused. No one would care for her except my husband and me. By the time I stopped nursing my husband started pressuring me to go to work. He continually abused me emotionally and verbally. How I stuck it out I will never know. I tried to stay focused on caring for my daughter and studying for my GED. I was thrilled when I received my certificate. I realized this was an amazing accomplishment because only one of my siblings at this time had a high school diploma.

During this time, I noticed a change in me. The love for my daughter started as a small flame burning deep within my being. I not only wanted to advocate for her but help my entire family. I began many conversations with my sisters regarding the sexual abuse we had experienced. The fallout from the abuse affected each of us in different ways, none of which were good.

There was also another change in me. I contemplated leaving my husband. I was sure I would end up dead if I stayed in the marriage. I had no choice but to go back to work when my daughter was three years old. I hid money as often as possible. I also purchased dishes, towels, and other needed items to prepare for my escape. I lived in constant fear and loneliness because I was lying and manipulating, hoping no one would know what I planned.

Work became my only place of normalcy. There I met a man who offered me attention and affection I was willing to take. No, we never had sex, but nevertheless it was an extramarital relationship. After four months, I realized I had to get some emotional help.

My husband and I had been married for four years when he went before the Elders regarding my infidelity. I was not disfellowshipped (which is being expelled and shunned), but I was publicly reprimanded. Imagine the elders going before the congregation and announcing that you have committed a wrongdoing. My husband was never disciplined for the emotional and physical abuse towards me. That too was swept under the rug. My husband was patted on back for his right to keep me in line. I was blamed for not being more submissive to him.

Feeling unloved, rejected, and shamed I took this opportunity to leave my husband and my religion. I knew this meant I would be leaving my entire family, but I was able to keep my daughter. When you leave the religion your family disowns you. I didn't know it at the time, but God was providing for me in unexplainable ways. He expected nothing from me and weaved opportunities throughout the coming days that would eventually lead me to Him.

I received a wonderful job offer that allowed me to provide for my daughter. Was everything perfect? Far from it. My life, like a spring capped so tightly and suddenly released, bounced everywhere. This was my life for the next several years. Everything was permissible. I thought being free to do whatever I wanted would bring peace. However, I soon learned that some choices are not what is best.

In my mid-twenties the mistakes I had made were too numerous to count. One regretful choice I made was my abortion. I can vividly remember the day I decided to drive up to the abortion clinic to ask questions. I had mentally gone back and forth a million times on making the decision. It was one of the most difficult choices of my life. I had met a man who had a lot to lose if I had the baby. We discussed the ramifications many times but neither of us knew what to do. He picked me up from my apartment that day. We both cried and once more reviewed our options. Is this really what we wanted to do? I didn't feel like I had another choice. I was a single mother and barely had enough money to keep my head above water. Another baby didn't seem like an option.

The waiting room was packed. I paused as I looked at the sign-in paper. Should I put my real name? Should I make one up? What if someone here knows me? The receptionist broke my stare, "Ma'am, just sign in and have a seat."

We sat silently among the many faces filled with despair. Once again, we grasped for clarity. We quietly discussed if this was what I wanted to do. WANTED? I don't know if I felt there was another option. They called my name.

The video was short but very persuasive. The nurse entered the room and asked, "Ready to get this done so you can go home?"

The only thing I remember was laying on the cold table with several people around me. The doctor asked, "Do you want to be awake for this?" "NO! ABSOLUTELY NOT!" I remember waking up feeling numb, frozen, and dead inside. The empowerment they promised me wasn't there. I got up and moved on with my life.

Moving on was difficult. I missed my family. Occasionally my mom and sisters were allowed to contact me because I never claimed another religion. The conversations were centered around them persuading me to come back to "the truth." In my reasoning, I knew Jehovah's Witnesses were the furthest thing from the truth. No persuasion on this earth would convince me to return.

I began studying as much as I could about God. While being a Jehovah's Witness, I was never allowed to read another Bible or other religious literature that wasn't issued by the JW's. I began to pray in a way that I'd never done before. I remember just screaming at God in anger one day and begging Him to give me an answer. I couldn't see He was orchestrating His plan for my life. He was working through others who knew Him.

I had a co-worker who befriended me, prayed for me in private and allowed me to be just be who I was. My boss and his wife became an example to me of what living as a Christian looked like. They were truly compassionate and exemplified Christ each day. I also met another friend who kept inviting me to church with her. I kept telling her no. Not because I didn't want to go, but because I knew if I stepped foot in another church my family would label me an "Apostate" (a person who renounces a religious belief) and have no choice but to disown me.

Months passed and I finally developed the courage to try their church. I can't explain the fear rising within me. I knew one thing. I was ready to do whatever it took to meet God or die trying. What I experienced was life-changing; the sweetest spirit was there. I didn't ask Jesus into my life that day – it took a lot of time, prayer, and surrendering my life to God. However, I did make another choice. I decided to come out publicly to my family as an "Apostate" in their religion. It took me two years to get up the courage.

I was the first in my family to stand up for the truth. My youngest sister has also left the JW religion. The rest of my family hasn't spoken to me over the past twenty years.

The day I accepted Jesus I knew I needed to understand God in a new way. It lit a fire within me. I began to study and research many different religions. Little by little I began to forgive myself and allow God to transform me. I didn't always make good choices but God used these difficult times to draw me closer to Him. He continued to bring the exact people I needed in my life to encourage me. This included therapists, church leaders, Christian friends, and many others.

Now I am a licensed professional counselor and biofeedback therapist. I enjoy studying the brain and how God intended for it to function. God daily renews my heart, mind, and soul. I can now be the person HE created me to be. I have a peace that settles my heart and slows my racing mind. I have learned to trust in Him concerning every aspect of my life and no longer run away from difficult circumstances or wade in fear.

I don't allow my past to define me. It certainly shaped me but Jesus used it to re-mold me; to help others, to receive healing, and live a life where I daily can proclaim, "I am brave!"

• • •

Brandii's story is a reminder that God is always reaching out to be in relationship with us. He waits patiently for us to acknowledge Him as our God. Just like Brandii, we experience God through a process of trusting Him. As we experience the truth of God's plan working in our lives, He will equip us to overcome every challenge this world can throw our way.

God wants you to be a powerful and strong person, not trembling like a frightened mouse. He knows that when you see the TRUTH of who He is, you'll be freed from the lies you've accepted as truth. Unlike Brandii's fears caused by condemnation, shame, and secrets, there is another fear which God considers necessary. We read in Leviticus 25:17 (ESV), "You shall not wrong one another, but you shall FEAR YOUR GOD, for I am the Lord your God."

This fear is a holy fear. God has instilled an inner feeling of respect to reverence Him as Lord. In this sense, God is known as "YAWEH," which means "Lord." This is the name God told Moses and the Israelites to use when referring to Him. It should go without saying that one who is given the ultimate authority or influence over our lives is very important. He deserves the utmost respect and worship.

God didn't create us to be afraid of Him. This sense of dreading or being apprehensive about His plan is a lie. God is the God of love not lies. Lies cause fear.

Fear drives a wedge between us and His love.

Why would He want that for us? We are told in His Word 365 times not to fear! That's one command for each day of the year.

Fear causes us to be consumed in worry and where there is fear of punishment, there can be no trust. But when there is a problem, God provides a way to overcome. By trusting in God—in YAWEH, —we can learn to be unafraid. Here are some scriptures telling us what God will do as we take time to get to know Him:

» God is with us. He will strengthen, help, and uphold us with his hand. – Isaiah 41:10
» God brings peace and guards our hearts. – Philippians 4:6-7
» God gives us His peace. – John 14:27
» God gives us power, love, and a sound mind. – 2 Timothy 1:7
» God gives us joy. – Psalm 94:19
» God has redeemed us, calls us by name, and states you are His. – Isaiah 43:1

…and the list goes on.

In other words, God is saying, "I am YOUR GOD."

When you open your heart to God, He will prove you have nothing to fear. Why? He has everything in control. He is the one true God; call upon Him and He will be there for you!

When we have a reverent fear of God our fears subside. We experience God's love. The Bible says this love, "casts out fear" (1 John 4:8) and "...removed our sins as far from us as the east is from the west" (Psalm 103:12).

Maybe you feel fearful of God because of what you've been taught by others or by a certain church affiliation. This is a lie. If the walls standing between you and God makes you feel condemned by your past; this is a lie too.

If you are in a church or religious group that doesn't follow the Word of God, I have one word of advice…

RUN!

Run straight into the arms of God! Everything you need to empower you to be an overcomer is freely given to those who accept the gift of God's love.

Sure, people are people. Individuals in high positions of authority are people too. You may have experienced some things along the way that have confused and even hurt you. This is not what God intended. He never intended for people to use their power to harm you. This is the very reason God wants to be in a relationship with you.

He wants to teach you boundaries to protect you and guide you with the TRUTH! He wants to show you how He has already conquered fear. He sent His one and only Son to die on the cross so you can have freedom and peace. We can pull up a chair, sit down with the one true God, and trust Him to knock down the walls.

One way to bring power into your life is through God's Word. You can take a verse and put your name within the Scripture. Here is a verse I recite often. God has not given (me) a spirit of fear, but of POWER,

LOVE, and a SOUND MIND! (2 Timothy 1:7 paraphrased).

*When God's Word penetrates your heart
and soul you will begin a new transformation.*

God has made provision for everyone. He made this sacrificial arrangement by giving His only Son, Jesus, because He knew we would choose selfish desires over Him. Sin was the choice that separated us from His presence.

Remember the scene in the first paragraph of this chapter? If you fear you will go to hell because you will never be acceptable to God, then check your underlying reason for this belief. Is it fear or pride?

Pride says, "I choose not to be in a relationship with God because I don't need Him. I can take care of myself." Fear says, "God won't accept me because of what I've done or what I am doing." I have good news for you if you lean towards the second. God doesn't need you to be perfect. He is the only one who is perfect. He knows you sin but wants you to know HE is HOLY and has made a way for you to be holy too. You may be thinking that is impossible.

From a human standpoint I would have to agree. As humans, it is impossible to please God. So, what is the point? If we can't please Him then we are destined to burn in the flames, correct? No! Absolutely not!

God became a man. Why? So, we could be holy. The Bible tells us, God is a Trinity. He is one God, but three persons. This is very difficult for us to understand but is a truth found in God's Word.

God is the Father who created the world. God is also the person, Jesus Christ, who sacrificed Himself so we could be freed from sin and be in a relationship with Him. God is a Spirit, too. His Spirit lives inside of our spirit when we invite Him to be in relationship with us. The Spirit gives us power to be successful in His mission.

Without God sending Jesus to offer His life in your place, you could never be holy. You could never receive God's presence to live inside your soul.

Doesn't this change the entire picture? Take a sip of that coffee and contemplate this moment.

Without His Spirit living in us, fear sneaks into the crevices in our hearts that are not protected by God. The enemy uses fear to wreak havoc in our lives and keeps us at a distance from God's love.

Fear says, "You can't!"

Fear shouts in your ears that you don't fit in the God-mold and says, "God will surely condemn me for the things I have done or the things I'm doing." You may feel you will never be good enough for God. God has a different perspective regarding YOU. If you sat down and said, "Hello" I think He would say something like this.

"I made you in the first place. I was the one that got you started. Don't be afraid! I have already started the process to redeem you. A process that doesn't happen overnight. A process that will continue through your entire lifespan. I came to rescue you from what you believe are your weaknesses and failings. Yes, it's me that has been calling you. I call you by your name. You are mine. When you are in over your head, I'm there with you. When you're between a rock and a hard place, you don't have to stay stuck there. And when you feel you are at the end of the rope, I'm there to catch you! Because I am God, your personal God, The Holy God of Israel, your Savior, I paid a big price for you. That's how much you mean to me! That's how much I love you! I'd sell off the whole world to get you back, trade everything just for you. So, don't be afraid"
(Isaiah 43:1-5 MSG paraphrased)

Jesus promised to leave "peace" with us (John 14:27 NIV), a peace the world can never give. Could it be that we have traded this peace for a life of fear? Could it be that we sit in fear pointing our finger unjustly in God's direction?

Fear may be what stands in the way of you having a relationship with God. However, when you say "Hello" to God, His power will begin to rise within you and empower you to stand up to the fears in your life. Again, this takes patience. It takes time a lot of us don't feel we have. This leads us to the next topic that can separate us from His presence—busyness. Not all walls are caused by trauma. Some we've placed there to keep things in perfect order. The more control we maintain, the more we believe things will go according to our plans. This too is a lie.

God

doesn't belong

on the last line of

your

"to-do" list.

He longs to be

the priority.

CHAPTER 5

WALL OF BUSYNESS

Look around you. I mean right now! Cell phone in hand. Television making mindless noise in the background. Computer on your lap and working at a job day in and day out. Calendar packed with kids' activities. Let's not forget your personal daily tasks like showering, laundry, cooking, and lawn care. All THINGS have the possibility of vying for your attention and standing in the way of you building a deep and personal relationship with God.

You may not be opposed to having a relationship with God. Yet in your search for satisfaction, you keep choosing things that are temporary. Things that take the place and fill up every part of your heart and mind, leaving no space for God. Money, fame, your "To Do List," and even relationships are things which take precedent over connecting with Him. Still here you are searching for peace, joy and anything that feels like real love.

How many times has God tried to call you out from this world into His presence? How many times has He given you opportunities to recognize who He is? Yet the busyness of life is the wall that blocks your view of Him. My friend Samantha knows firsthand about the wall of Busyness.

Samantha

In the fall of 2018, I was sitting on my couch with my computer strategically placed on top of my seven-month pregnant belly. There

I worked to dig myself out of an unending pile of work emails while watching (aka helping) my two-year-old line up every tractor, truck, and train along our cherry-walnut chest my papa made me as a wedding present. The oven's high-pitched beep indicated our one-sheet pan dinner was ready as I motioned to my friend to come on in and drop off the Camelback sippy cup my son had left at her house the day before.

I was swimming in chaos but could feel myself sinking. My shoulders sagged, my eyes closed, and I slumped down on the couch just trying to block out my unending to-do list. Busy was the norm and hurried was my routine. I spent my days jumping from one task to the next, working tirelessly to mark off every item on my list.

By evening I was exhausted. I walked down the worn pathway to the mailbox and my ever-inquisitive next-door neighbor casually asked how things were going. I responded like I normally did, "Oh, I'm good, busy…but good." Her response is what stuck with me. She said, "I just don't know how you do it all."

Her words felt like a badge of honor. They meant she was impressed with how much I could do and how I was achieving more. My ugly, selfish pride surged.

However, in the stillness of the night, the Lord's conviction came raining down as my sweet neighbor's words echoed in my mind.

"I just don't know how you do it all."

Those few words weren't a badge of honor, they were a call to action. They were an indication that my life was full of misplaced priorities. I was striving but never satisfied. I was failing to do what God had called me to do and falling short of what God had called me to be.

When I was six years old, I sat with my parents in my room reading an evangelical pamphlet. I was familiar with what the pamphlet said because I would go with my parents on weekly church visitation. I asked the Lord to save me and I have no doubt He did that night. However, it's taken me years of walking with the Lord to effectively combat this need for busyness and control.

My family jokes that we are all plagued by the "responsibility bug."

For several generations I've watched as members of my family give of themselves, perfect their tasks, and tirelessly work because they have a responsibility to do so. I'm part of this group.

From the time I can remember as the oldest child in my family of five, I've been a Type-A perfectionist. In school I was the one everyone depended on to lead the group project. In times of play I was always the one in charge; dictating the game, enforcing the rules, and ensuring everything went to plan. As I aged, this love for control grew.

Not only did I have a need for control, but I had a need to be busy. Multi-tasking, time-management, and planning were more than just practices I put into place -- they had become character traits.

God used that night to gently inform me this "busy life" had become an idol. As I placed my plans and priorities above all, I was missing something. I had failed to place my day in His hand and align my timetable with His. I was missing peace and joy.

I knew I had to learn to lay down my desire to pursue financial security, job success, do-it-all parenting and endless pleasures over the commands and will of God. This doesn't mean I could never make plans or multi-task. It doesn't mean I say no to anything and everything. And, it doesn't mean I'm allowed to become slothful or lazy. It does mean I make myself available to the Lord and His plan above all.

God began to meet me where I was and work within my schedule and circumstances as I let Him. I learned to surrender my schedule and open my eyes to all God was doing around me. This pursuit to strip away busyness wasn't made up of big, dramatic changes or revolutionary ideas. It was made up of day-to-day, moment-by-moment decisions to lay aside my plans, my control, and my desires.

Recently, my family moved to another suburb in Oklahoma. Even though change is never easy, I'm so grateful the Lord had taught me how to slow down and live unhurried because I trusted He was placing us exactly where He needed us.

As soon as we found our new house we began praying for our neighbors and were determined to meet every person on our street within the first few weeks of moving in. I had my kids help me bake cookies and we delivered them with cards containing our phone numbers and hand written messages to let them know we were praying for them.

As days went on this new community God had placed us in began to develop. We became what we call "front-porch people." My husband built me a beautiful porch swing and I would sit outside praying for neighbors to come out with their kids, or check their mail, or take their trash out. When they did, I tried to have a conversation.

As I've developed relationships, I've been able to invite neighbors to church and Bible study. My husband and I have shared our testimonies and have been encouraged in return.

I'm still Type-A, still love to plan, and still find myself busy. But as I pursue the Lord daily, He's taught me to slow down, look for His opportunities, and rest in who He is. I never want anything to come before my love for God. I've learned that the more I have intimate conversations with Him and search for His will in all my decision making, the more I have peace and joy that only He can give.

• • •

The problem with busyness is universal. More time is spent on everything, but little time is spent for what is most important. Before long, your thoughts are filled with anxiousness and your relationships begin to suffer. You may begin to feel guilty as your mind and body cry out for some rest. Whether you're a Type-A personality like Samantha or you have a hyper-active brain like me, rest will never come without making time for God to direct you into a place of balance.

I often wonder how I get to this place where everything in my life seems to be controlled by outside forces instead of me being the leader of my own calendar. Even when my intentions are optimal, I find myself wondering what creature snuck in my back door and filled my calendar with stuff. I feel guilty because I know my time with God suffers and falls into the "so-so" relationship category. *God doesn't want a "so-so" relationship.*

He wants you to experience Him with complete abandonment. He knows that when you experience His love you will never have to search again for something authentic! Why? Because His love is overwhelming and miraculous; nothing in this world can compare.

Because we are human, we sometimes choose church or religion to begin to replace intimate moments with God. Don't get me wrong. I love going to worship with my church family but church is not meant to replace my daily walk with God.

Some people go to church for social activities which only adds to the busyness. God calls us to attend church for instruction and worship with the body of Christ. However, if you are attending church to replace intimate conversations with God you are only building another wall that will end in disappointment.

God is a Spirit. He lives inside the spirit of His followers. When you invite Jesus to come and live inside your spirit, a soul-altering experience transpires between you and your Creator. This transformation is to connect you to your God and Savior.

However, if we go to church only to minimize guilt or for others to assume we are a Christian, we will find ourselves searching once again. Ultimately, we have traded an intimacy with God for religion.

Going to church doesn't solidify your relationship with Jesus. First, "church" is not a building. God tells us in the scriptures that the church is made up of people. People with a desire to be in relationship with Jesus, learn more about Him, and hang out to support and encourage each other in their walk with Christ. This statement may not be what most Christians want to hear…

Going to church does not make a relationship with God.

If you go to church or are considering visiting a church: you are going to fellowship, worship God with other Christian believers, and learn more about Him. Church helps us develop a relationship with God, especially in the early stages.

If you are going to church because you think this is how you receive a relationship with God, your expectations will bring about disappointment. Building a relationship with God must be intimate – between you and God, not just about going to church. The church doesn't save you.

Jesus tells a story about a person that had heard about Him in Luke 8:14, yet the relationship didn't develop. In fact, busyness was the cause that the relationship did not mature.

"The seeds that fell among the thorns represent those who hear the message, but all too quickly the message is crowded out by the cares and riches and pleasures of this life. And they never grow into maturity."

Oh Lord! Don't let this ever be me again! Yes, I've been there and done that. I have traded a personal relationship with God for a Step One, Two, Three sort of religion. You know my story. The result wasn't pretty, not pretty at all.

God wants to remind us that He is aware of "things" that vie for our attention. Solomon, a very wise man warns us: *"Guard your heart above all else, for it determines the course of your life"(Proverbs 4:23).* When God enters our spirit, we must guard our hearts from anything that would deter us from our relationship with Him.

Having a successful relationship with Jesus requires work. If you google "ways to have successful relationships" you will find lists of things to make it happen. Here are a few…

> » Make the relationship a priority. Offer time to express your love and adoration.
> » Be truthful and open regarding all aspects of your life, especially the ugly stuff.
> » Express your needs and fears – be vulnerable.

I have one more to add to the list…

Love with all your heart, mind, soul, and strength.

If this isn't accomplished in whatever relationship you are investing in, love will stay superficial and most likely end up non-existent.

We see many examples of individuals that were in a relationship with God in the Bible. All these people weren't always successful in the relationship. However, when the relationship was healthy and strong, you see extraordinary things happen in and around their lives. What was the key? Jesus said two things were most important to be successful in a relationship with Him.

These two commandments are in Matthew 22:35-40. Here we see Jesus' response when asked what was the greatest commandment.

"You must love the Lord your God with all your heart,
all your soul, and all your mind."

This is the first and greatest commandment. A second is equally important.

"Love your neighbor as yourself.
The entire law and the demands of the prophets
are based on these two Commandments."

Jesus placed the relationship with God as the top priority. The second is our relationship with others. He said you must LOVE! Love God first with everything you have and then love those you have relationships with. PERIOD!! How easy is that? Loving God should be easy, right? Not exactly!

Remember? Relationships are difficult! Especially when you place so many things before the one you love and are longing to have a relationship with. Jesus says He doesn't just want your heart (feelings). He also wants to develop your soul (go deeper), your mind (thoughts) and don't forget

Mark 12:30 added strength (with everything you've got) in his gospel.

Everything will revolve around God when He remains the priority in your life. The more you humble yourself and allow Him to be a part of all areas of your life, the more you'll experience the amazing power of His love.

The second commandment becomes more natural after you accomplish the first. God's love saturates you and then overflows into the lives of others! The more you allow Him to pour His love into your life; the more you will experience how powerful His love really is.

It's like when you fell in love for the first time. Sure, maybe it wasn't true love, but those goosebumps you got every time the person came around were the real deal. What did you do? You started talking to everyone you knew about the person.

You were excited to know everything about the person and wanted everyone to be as excited as you were. Your friends probably got tired of you talking about your new love. You didn't care! Why? You were experiencing feelings of infatuation that led to love!

Unfortunately, most first love experiences don't last. In fact, they aren't really love at all. It would be truer to say that you were falling in fondness. Why don't they last? It's usually because one or both people involved are not mature and determined enough to maintain the work that is required to establish a strong, enduring relationship.

However, when you have a relationship that is worth working on and your love matures, watch out!

The same is true with your relationship with God. There is no stopping what God wants to do in your life! Remember the plan? He will teach you and transform you into His likeness. His power will be released to help transform the lives of others with which you are in contact.

Will this life be perfect by having a relationship with Christ? Truthfully, no! The Christian life will still have trials and hardships. The difference is God's presence will be with you every step of the way. You can '*experience God's peace, which exceeds anything we can understand*' (Philippians 4:7 NLT). This is a promise of God to those who have relationship with Him!

Jesus told his disciples, "I have loved you even as the Father has loved me. Remain in my love. When you obey my commandments, you remain in my love, just as I obey my Father's commandments and remain in his love. I have told you these things so that you will be filled with joy. Yes, your JOY WILL OVERFLOW! - John 15:9 NLT.

That is what we all want right? JOY! Who would refuse that? *Joy comes from being deeply rooted and receiving inspired happiness that only comes from God.*

We have now looked at three strongholds: rejection, fear, and busyness. These strongholds may keep us distant and unable to build a deep relationship with God. You can easily see we need His help.

The length of time spent on this part of your journey is personal. It depends on the amount of time you set aside to work on getting to know God. This is a choice that is left up to you. I can personally attest to these facts. The more conversations you have with God about your insecurities, weaknesses, and what you want to achieve in your life, the more likely you will experience His power.

The more vulnerable you are, the more you will feel freedom to sit in His presence. And the more thankful you are, the more compassionate you become. Like any relationship, the more you feel you are accepted for who you are, the more easily you can trust His unchanging love for you.

This brings us to the next topic. Do you have feelings of unworthiness? Are you a people-pleaser or do you struggle with fear of failure? If you answered 'yes' to any of these questions, you may already know you lean against the next wall.

Are you tired?

Are you worn out?

Burned out on religion?

Come to me.

Get away with me

and you'll recover your life.

Learn the unforced

rhythms of grace.

Matthew 11:28-30

CHAPTER 6

WALL OF PERFECTIONISM

When I was five years old, I had a red dress with large pockets in the front. I loved to wear it because I could stuff lots of treasures inside the pockets and carry them with me throughout the day. When it was time to take a bath and get ready for bed, my mom would lift the dress over my head and all my trinkets would spill to the floor. We would hurriedly pick them up in a towel and my mom would carry them to my room so I could finish the task at hand.

Perfectionism is like an outfit with many pockets. Your shirt pocket carries people-pleasing trinkets while another is full of things causing fear. The one on your left back hip is packed with performance-based feelings while the one on your right is filled with thoughts causing low self-esteem. In most cases, you don't even realize your pockets are so jammed packed with the weight of perfectionism mentalities until your mind short circuits and everything comes spilling out.

That was me. I was the youngest of three siblings. I worked hard to please and obey my parents. I wanted to please my friends, too. I always strived to be in the "good-girls" group. I loved helping others and serving in church and was always appreciated and praised for my efforts. I people-pleased my way till I was exhausted. What was the problem? My expectation was unrealistic for what I thought I needed to be.

Making good choices and following the rules are wonderful attributes if done for the right reasons. But when expectations are too high, they can cause emotionally instability. The life of excellence we strive for is nothing more than a constant cycle of failed ambition.

Our next story is shared by Megan. Her idea of knowing God had to do with being good. But when everything fell apart, she found her striving to be perfect was not enough.

Megan

Crying left me exhausted. I could make no sense of what was happening. This wasn't part of my plan. I gently laid my son in his bed and my worry grew with each rise and fall of his chest. I reached to hang the last article of clothing in my closet as my knees buckled beneath me and my body collapsed to the floor. The anger and hurt bottled up for years gushed as I cried out to God in desperation.

I grew up in a small town. My parents worked hard and held high expectations for my sister and me. We were very close and did most things together. We ate dinner around the table and went to church most Sundays and Wednesdays like clockwork. I learned about God at an early age. I was saved and baptized when I was in the seventh grade. Summers held many happy memories for our family. We would travel to the lake for water sports and cookouts. We laughed till our stomachs ached and then played car games on the drive home.

My mom and dad made sure we had everything we needed to succeed. They were consistent and set rules they expected us to follow. I grew up wanting to please them and worked hard to accomplish the goals they set for me.

Perfection and organization are etched deep in my brain: a blessing and a curse. The skills I learned from them helped me in my career but caused problems in my relationships. My internal drive to make everything perfect was constantly in active mode. I wanted everyone to be happy and did everything I could do to please them. I was bound to fail, right? I feared failure more than anything.

My parents were great at being present and telling us they loved us. However, my family showed little outward affection. For me, physical touch was an unfilled cup. So, when boys started showing me attention, I liked it. I started dating a boy my age when I was fifteen. He made me feel beautiful and perfect. He said all the right things to draw me in. He was kind to me and loved to hold hands and hug me. The sweet compliments and words of affection slowly turned to guilt-filled comments pressuring me to do more. I found it difficult to speak my mind and stand up for myself. I lost my virginity before I turned sixteen.

By this point I knew the relationship was toxic, but I had given him something I was only supposed to give to one person - - my future husband. I wanted the relationship to end, but I felt obligated to stay with him. I knew my behavior was wrong and longed to confide in my parents but was afraid to ask for help.

My boyfriend came over one Friday without my parent's knowledge. We were crossing lines physically when my dad came home early and caught us. I was devastated because I had over stepped their authority.

There was little discussion about what I did. My parents took my vehicle away from me, leaving me to deal with small-town gossip. The truck was my pride and joy and everyone knew it. Kids at school asked me what happened when they saw me in an older vehicle. I would only say I got in trouble. I felt I had let so many people down, especially my parents. Mentally I labeled myself the bad kid. I perceived my relationship with my parents had changed too. We had no further discussion about the incident. I just tried to cope and deal with the consequences of my bad choice the best I could. It was traumatic for me. I slowly pulled away from my parents; our relationship was strained.

I then began dating a guy from high school who was older than me. He was great and never pressured me to go further than I felt comfortable. I felt so adored as our relationship grew. When he went to college, we stayed together. But when it came time for me to choose a college I was in a predicament. Choose the college my parents wanted me to go to or where my boyfriend attended. My parents had made almost every major decision for me. This time I chose what I wanted instead of what they wanted. Again, I felt I had let them down.

Staying at the college lasted, but the relationship with my boyfriend ended. Immediately after our break-up, I began to date someone I had known since high school. I had always had a crush on him. He had all the charm, the drive for hard work, and seemed to check all the boxes: great family, my parents loved him, and he was family-oriented. Everything seemed great, but looking back, I had ignored the red flags.

From the beginning we did all the things that he wanted to do. I felt disappointed. I worried I was giving up college experiences to spend time with him but I was eager to please. During my senior year in college, most of my friends planned to marry as soon as they graduated. I wanted this too. I had invested two years being with him and assumed this was the plan for us. He was work-focused and decided to open a business in his hometown. I had to choose him or the career path I had worked for; I chose him.

Almost one year after graduating from college I began to have doubts and feelings of failure. I messaged a friend my worries. "I'm tired of feeling unimportant to him. Either we get engaged, or I'm moving on." He saw the message and randomly proposed to me. Looking back on the situation I'm still unsure why his motivation to marry had done a three-sixty, but everything I dreamed of was coming to fruition and this was what I wanted. Still, deep inside I knew something was wrong.

I had already had suspicions of his interest in other girls and had seen text conversations that I felt were inappropriate. When I would find something out it was always at an inopportune time to discuss the matter. Sometimes we were with my parents or hanging out with other friends. I didn't want to make a scene. When we did discuss it, he worked to convince me I was over-reacting so I would eventually choose to dismiss the argument. He would say it wasn't what it seemed and it wouldn't happen again.

We went ahead and got married; it didn't stop.

You may wonder why I chose to marry him. I loved him. We had good times together. Plus, my list of why I "should" marry him was longer than the "shouldn't" list. We had spent years building a relationship together. I didn't want to start over and the maternal clock was ticking. I was twenty-three and thought I'd be an old maid if I didn't get married. Besides, marriage was in my plan. This is what was supposed to happen, right?

My only reservation was being convinced of his promiscuity. I thought because he was marrying me, he loved me enough to stop crossing the line. I thought we could get past this. I was wrong, again. I would think things were getting better only to find some tidbit of information that would cause mistrust in our relationship. He'd make promises and I wanted to believe him. The emotional toll and constant worry caused an enormous strain on me. I had little trust in him and he didn't feel I would ever be happy.

Four years into our marriage I became pregnant. I was naive to think being pregnant would change the situation. Even though I was ready for a child, he wasn't. It seemed he didn't want to touch me. The more pregnant I became, the more I felt he wanted to connect with anyone else besides me.

When my son was born, I noticed a shift in my feelings. When I would hold him in my arms, all I could think about was protecting him. I decided I would make some changes in myself and began investing more time in church. The pastor had a way of connecting the Bible to life experiences in a significant way. I began to grow in my understanding of God and His Word. I felt safe and loved when I attended church.

Stress in life escalated a couple of years after my son was born. The business my husband started failed. I felt compassion for his situation. I leaned into the relationship and tried hard to make things work. I helped him dissolve the business by taking out personal loans to cover the debt. We downsized our house, got rid of our cars, and tried to start over.

Only three months after making those sacrifices, I found he was still crossing lines with someone from the past even though I had repeatedly asked him to stop. After seven years of marriage and realizing I would never be able to stop his affairs, I stood in the doorway between the utility room and the garage with a two-year-old on my hip and told him to leave. The next few days, I was an emotional wreck!

I cried out to God, asked for forgiveness, and begged for help. In a surreal moment a calm blanket of clarity rested over me. The life I had known for the past eleven years had ended, but God had a plan.

The next few months were an emotional rollercoaster ride, from telling my parents to filing for divorce. Yet through everything, God kept me calm. The divorce was over and my life started over too. Through every step, I knew God had everything in control. What I thought would be an unmanageable and scary event became a fresh beginning.

My relationship with God began to change too. I spent many nights on the floor of my closet and the blanket of peace remained. I still had to endure those angry individuals around me holding mental-pitchforks and ready for battle, but God was standing in the middle of it all. He fought the opposition for me and led me out of the destruction, filled with hope and strength. He helped me make choices without fear of failing and revealed HIS plan for my son and me!

I still experience the fallout of what happened during those tumultuous years, but I'm stronger now. I am better about realizing I can't please everyone. I don't have to be perfect.

I'm engaged now! He understands my past and allows me to be myself. My fiancé has a son, too. We work together raising our sons.

I have learned to TRUST in God to take care of me. He has taught me the meaning of grace in my weakness. I don't have to worry because He is always with me and still provides the blanket of peace when I cry out to Him.

• • •

Like Megan, many suffer from perfectionism. Thomas Curran and Andrew P. Hill wrote an article in 2018, *Perfectionism Is Increasing, and That's Not Good News.* They stated, "Perfectionism is a misleading trait. It promises meticulousness, hard work, and dedication but, although it can deliver motivation and performance, also delivers mental health difficulties. Our research suggests that perfectionism is increasing. Expect the frequency of these difficulties to do the same."[8]

Individuals who struggle with perfectionism may also struggle in their relationships. They find it difficult to trust others and often feel they can never measure up. If this is the wall that you struggle with, you may also find it seeps over into your relationship with God.

Jesus said, "But you are to be perfect, even as your Father in heaven is perfect." Wait a minute. That's impossible! You are correct. You may be thinking it's impossible to be perfect like God. So, what was Jesus saying?

Just before the verse where He uses the word "perfect" He states He came to "fulfill" the requirement God had for us to be perfect through the Law (Matthew 5:17). In the eyes of God, Jesus' sacrifice made us perfect. God doesn't see the sin in us because Jesus' blood has washed us white as snow. We are then in the process of being sanctified, or set apart as being holy, as we finish the fight imperfectly until we see His face. Then, we will be perfect. We will be like him. (1 John 3:2).

I believe our most life-altering moment with God arrives when we are at our weakest. There in the pit of our imperfection, we get the true glimpse of His love for us. In our moments of weakness, He reveals He is greater. Megan's relationship with God was based on religion until she needed a Savior. She hadn't experienced His transforming power until she was unable to fix her problems herself. In that humbling moment, she released control and cried out to God. He did what He always does, accepted her just like she was.

If you struggle with perfectionism, God is waiting to reveal Himself to you and allow you to experience His rhythm of grace. All you need to do is ask. The next wall is one of the toughest to identify and conquer. But remember, nothing is impossible for God!

The moment

your prideful heart dies;

you make space

for the God of your heart.

CHAPTER 7

WALL OF PRIDE

Do you choose other things in your life to place before your time with God? We all do. It's because of CHOICE. That is also why there is evil. Bad decisions are often made without realizing the snowball effect that is to come. The negative experiences that come from prideful choices are overwhelming.

In the Garden, God could have done away with choice and then there wouldn't be evil, right? *But without choice we could never experience authentic love.*

God created us to experience His love and He wants to experience ours. He knew unless He gave the opportunity of choice, our love would just be counterfeit. He wanted us to choose Him. He longs for us to place Him first above everything else in our lives.

I shared my story in Chapter 2. The revelation God gave me concerning the circumstances leading to me making such poor decisions was eye-opening. I was prideful, I sinned, and there was no going back and fixing what I did. However, God doesn't leave us there wallowing in the mud of our disgrace.

As I humbled myself to Him, He showed me that His plan was not interrupted, not in the least. From hundreds of examples in His Word, He also showed me that I was still part of His plan. He wants you to know that you are part of His plan too. The problem is most people don't identify that the main wall between them and God is usually one of pride.

Pride is a disposition or attitude that affects the way that you conduct yourself. Not all pride is bad. It can be positive too. For instance, being proud of your children or completing something you have worked very hard to achieve is a form of pride. However, pride in spiritual terms nearly always leads to our downfall. You can think of it as a slow, downward spiral toward everything that is not part of a relationship with God.

When I first began to research spiritual pride, an article caught my attention entitled, *41 Evidences of Pride by Nancy Demoss Wolgemuth.*[9] I admit I recognized a few of these items working in my life. I had to check my heart in each of these areas and ask myself why I felt uncomfortable as my eyes traveled down the list. Here are just a few:

> » Selfishness: My time, property, money, etc. is more important to me than God.
> » Thinking excessively about SELF: I spend more time thinking and worrying about my outer appearance and what others think about me, instead of what God thinks about me.
> » Placing self above others: I think I am smarter and/or get annoyed with people that know less than me.
> » Self-centered: I need everything to revolve around me. I keep trying to direct everything back to the way I want it.
> » Spiritual perfectionism: I think I am more spiritual than others. I put others down when their faith is weak or they are at a different place in their journey than me.
> » Non-teachable: I get irritated when someone tries to teach me something from God's Word.
> » Always right: I try to prove people wrong.
> » Defensive: I attack back when questioned or confronted.
> » Struggle admitting wrong: I struggle admitting wrong and find it difficult to ask for forgiveness when I have wronged or caused hurt in another's life.
> » Criticize: I name call or put people down in actions or words.

» Fear or worry: I obsess a lot because I depend on my
   own abilities.
» Minimal Prayer: I depend more on myself and don't ask
   God for help.

Okay, be honest. Were one or more from the list jumping out at you? Recognize these areas and take them seriously. The problem with all of these is the amount of focus that is placed on self instead of God. *The more time spent on the "I" is less time spent on developing a relationship with God.* The more time spent on what we DESIRE and what we DESERVE, the less time we spend depending on God. *If we are not having a relationship with God, how can we walk in His plan for our lives?*

Pride is a huge thick wall. Unless we can identify and admit that pride is the culprit, we can never know God. Pride says I'm not even sure if I need God. I have handled everything just fine myself up to this point.

Please don't let this offend you. We are human. It is natural for us to struggle here. In fact, pride is such a stronghold it is mentioned forty-six times in God's Word. Yep! It's a major struggle for most of us. What it all boils down to is this:

Pride says, "I've got this! I don't need you God."

If you don't feel you need God this will always limit the depth of relationship you can have with Him.

The worst characteristic of pride is how sneaky it is. You may not even realize it has creeped up on you, wrapped its ugly, bony fingers around your neck and tossed you about like a rag doll. Tossed you right in the dirt for you to deal with the fallout of your own bad choices.

That was me. Let me emphasize something in that statement. That *was* me. Yes, God forgave me and pulled me out of the pit, but the consequences of my choices were not so easy for me to overcome. And even today over twenty-three years later, the fallout sometimes haunts me.

Have you been there? Made a really bad decision that left you wide open for the devil to haunt you with guilt and shame?

Well, let me promise you that if you build a relationship with God, a deep and lasting relationship with Him, He will be your defender and show you victory over your past.

This brings me to introduce you to another friend of mine. I first met Tessa at an appointment at the eye doctor's office where she worked. I was immediately drawn to her. She was very helpful and friendly. I know this is the reason many patients loved coming to that office. She answered every question I had and worked hard to make sure everyone was satisfied.

When I started my first Bible study, I was thrilled when she showed up. Several girls met at a nearby coffee shop. The topic was, *"Do you believed in God?"* Everyone gave a response as we went around the table. Tessa's was "I believe in God and pray all the time." She only attended twice, but every time I visited the eye doctor, we would catch up.

Two years later, I heard the horrible news about an accident she was involved in. I was heartbroken and feared the impending outcome for Tessa.

I love Tess! I love that she is willing to share her story with you. It is open. It is raw. It is shocking. It may cause some feelings you aren't aware of to stir within you. Maybe even some judgmental feelings toward her. So, beware! Check your heart and make sure pride doesn't creep up on you. Check and make sure as you read this story you don't think you are too spiritual to make a wrong choice, are a better person than Tessa, or even find yourself shaking your head in disbelief. Instead, I hope you will see Tessa with a humble heart. Know we are all susceptible to making choices that can destroy us and others. But with God, a new life is always possible.

I am extremely humbled that she would open her heart to give you a glimpse into what God is doing in her life. A life in which most freedom has been stripped away because of choices she made that unfortunately can't be reversed.

Tessa

Court day was the beginning of a new journey for me. The sentence was handed down. I certainly wasn't prepared. Who would be? My heart sank, my mind fell into shock, and I could do nothing more than breathe. I knew I was responsible for all my actions. I have never been one to blame anyone else for the choices I've made. I found it easy to scrutinize everything about myself. What I found made me miserable.

The behaviors that sent me to this place behind the concrete walls brought shame. I hated the person I had become and found myself in the darkest place I had ever been in emotionally, mentally, and physically. How I wished I could go to sleep and wake up to find it was all a horrible dream.

As a child, I learned very little about God and Jesus. I mainly thought if I did bad things, I would go to hell. I often felt inferior and unworthy. My grandma who was the main caregiver told me that at the age of five I said, "There are people under my bed that say I'm not good enough." In my little mind, I thought I was the reason my parents were absent from my life.

My mom, who was single, was absent for most of my childhood and my teenage years. I learned how to take care of myself the best I could. She was physically present, but rarely mentally or emotionally present. When I was nine years old, we lived with my grandparents. One day my mom brought a man to the house for introductions. Not long after, she announced she was pregnant and would be moving into an apartment with him.

I didn't want to move away from my grandparents' love and care, but I had no choice. In the beginning things seemed okay with my mom and her boyfriend, but alcohol soon reared its ugly head. When my sister was a toddler, I became her babysitter at night. I resented my mother's choice for not shouldering the responsibility of taking care of her own baby. Remember, I was only nine years old. I also feared the after-bar drunken fights between my mom and her husband. This also fueled my bitterness.

I began running away to my grandparent's house, but my mom would always pick me up and take me back home. The marriage didn't last long. My mom eventually found a twenty-year old to come to our apartment and babysit. She would bring her kids and her boyfriend. Their attention was rarely on us, which left us unsupervised. This led me to experiment with promiscuous behavior and alcohol for the first time. I didn't like how it tasted but drank until I was drunk. I became so sick I swore to never drink again. Unfortunately, I continued to hang around other kids who were dabbling in alcohol. This led to drinking more often. I was a mess.

My promiscuity led to a pregnancy at the age of fifteen. My second child was born twelve months later. My relationships ended as quickly as they began and left me searching for love. I was hurting and filled with an enormous amount of disappointment. Alcohol and drugs numbed the loss, pain, and insecurity I was unable to deal with at such a young age.

The adult "me" believed I was in control of everything in my life. My self-centered, self-serving attitude was negative at best. I still believed those voices from my childhood and chose destructive habits to deal with the pain. Drinking alcohol had become a self-made prison. I sometimes wondered how I could drink and still go to work. I believed I could always manage; sober or not. Even after marrying and having more children, I never fully realized the pain I was causing my family and myself. I never imagined that so many lives would be forever changed because of the negative choices I made.

Thinking about the bad things I had done only confirmed my belief about not being good enough. It confirmed that going to hell happens to bad people. That's why I ended up here in prison, right? I know you are wondering what brought me to this place. I am here because tragically I killed a man in a car accident. This horrific memory will forever be a part of my life and thoughts. There will never be a day I won't wish things could be different. That is something I can never change no matter how badly I want to.

After the accident, there were family and friends who tried to help. My boss knew my heart and continued to allow me to work until the court date. My friend and co-worker spent many hours trying to encourage me. Others helped me with court costs and another dear friend drove me to appointments. There were many moments I was hanging on by a thread. I tried to do my best to treasure each moment knowing it could be my last for a long time. I attended my son's graduation from military service and held my new grandson. My husband stuck by me through the extreme amount of stress surrounding our lives. I dreaded the point these freedoms would not be available to me.

I never dreamed my life story would include a chapter which took place in prison. Yet, this will be my life for many years to come. Since I first arrived here, there are many things I wish I never had to face:

Friends I thought were friends, no longer write.
My husband and people I thought loved me,
didn't hang on.
Prison is very lonely.

I decided I needed Someone greater than me who could give me strength and vision for my future. I began attending every church service available and wrote to many churches to send me Bible studies. The church services were uncomfortable at first. The same feelings of "not being good enough" made me feel like I didn't belong.

Sitting there on those church pews, my heart and mind were filled with so many emotions. As I listened to the sermons, participated in worship singing, and prayed for those dear to me, I realized Jesus was the One I needed. I learned He came to the earth to die for my sins. Wow! He sacrificed everything for me. I was drawn to reading my Bible more and more. During one service, I went to the front to pray and accepted Jesus Christ as my Savior and Lord of my life. Now, I am truly free; forgiven.

Prison is very difficult. I face all daily challenges with God by my side. The Bible says that God will take things meant for evil and use them for good. Now, I can say that this is true. I have a few friends who continue to send me letters of encouragement, Bible studies, visit, and pray for me. I am thankful for those who donate needed clothing items when I can receive them.

I've learned I have zero control over my life. I am learning to trust God each day, hour, and minute. Sometimes I try to take back control because it feels more comfortable; old patterns are hard to break. When I doubt, God shows me He is working for my good.

God knows the motives of my heart and I must keep my thoughts on Him. I know He has a plan for me beyond these walls. However, I have learned I must be thankful for who I am today. I hold to the promise that He is always with me, even in this place within the concrete walls.

• • •

Visiting Tessa behind bars in prison is a catch 22. You are thrilled to see her, but sad about the fact she will be in prison for many years to come. The first time I went to visit her, she revealed that even though she believed in God, she didn't have a personal relationship with Jesus.

We recalled the Bible studies she attended where she thought saying she believed in God was enough. However, if reading the Bible, praying a million prayers, and just saying, "I believe there is a God" were enough; then reading a marriage guide, telephoning your spouse several times a day and saying, *I believe you are great guy* would be enough to make a strong and lasting marriage.

The truth is you can know there is a God, yet not be in relationship with Him. You can also know scriptures in the Bible but not know the God behind the Bible. God's Word tells us if we are not in relationship with God, we are living in pride. Where does pride lead to? To a fall.

In Tessa's story we see her living independently from God. She was living life disconnected from God which made her a vulnerable target to attacks from Satan. Having the ability of choice made her susceptible to making bad decisions.

If you knew Tessa personally and hadn't heard her story, you would say she is a loving, hard-working, and intelligent women. You would have never in your wildest imagination believed that she would end up serving a very long prison sentence. You might even say that because of one bad choice, she should have received grace from the court. However, it wasn't because of one bad choice. Tessa had strongholds in her life. She was controlled by huge walls of mistrust, dependency issues, and pride that controlled her.

If you have problems with drugs or alcohol, you know how hard it is to overcome them. Especially, when you are fighting alone. That is why everyone needs a Savior. Everyone needs the power of the Holy Spirit inside them.

> *Head knowledge doesn't replace the power of*
> *God's Spirit dwelling in our lives.*
> *A relationship with Jesus is what empowers*
> *us to be overcomers.*

Maybe you are thinking," I would never make choices that bad." Allow me to enlighten you! People that make bad choices have often said those same words many times.

> *Pride like all sin, weaves its way into your heart*
> *and settles there hoping you will be destroyed.*

Even if you feel pride would never make you fall "that bad," pride is still pride. When a person says, "I can handle my life myself," they are telling God, "I don't need you." Let's look at another example of pride from the storyteller of all storytellers.

Jesus loved to teach principles through stories also known as parables. He talked about the proud in Luke 18:9-14. Here is my paraphrased version.

Two men went to a church to pray. One man was obsessed with being perfect and holier than others. The other man knew little about

God, yet confessed he sinned greatly.

As they knelt, the perfect man prayed, "God thank you I am not greedy, dishonest, and unfaithful in marriage like other people. I am so glad that I am not like this other man that has come to pray. I go without food for not one, but two days a week and I give you a tenth of all I earn. Amen."

Then the sinner who knelt in the distance hung his head low. He thought he was not good enough to look toward heaven. He was so sorry for all he had done and began to cry and beat on his chest. He prayed, "God please have pity on me! I am such a sinner."

Then Jesus stated that when the two men went home it was the sinner, not the perfect man who pleased God.

If you put yourself above others, you will be low in God's eyes.
But, if you humble yourself, you will be honored by God!

How do you think God sees you? Well, let me tell you. God sees you exactly where you are. Only you can decide if you need God. Only you can decide if you want God.

This brings us full circle. This brings us back to the discussion of relationship. When you ask God to be in a relationship with you, any walls that stand in the way must be destroyed for the relationship to develop and become strong. How do you do that? Funny you should ask.

YOU don't do a thing.
What? Are you serious? I'm totally serious.
GOD must be the One to knock down the walls.

That's right! Jesus already destroyed the walls when He gave His life for you. He already freed you from a life of sin. His blood covered your sin. He already provided His Spirit to enter your soul and become one with your spirit when He rose from the dead and returned to God the Father.

When you say to Jesus, I believe in you and want to follow you, the foundation of the wall begins to shake. When you say, I am sorry for sinning against you by believing I didn't need you, the concrete shifts. And when you say, Jesus, I believe you died, rose, and are preparing a place for me to live with you for eternity, the stones crumble. God destroys the walls and gives you freedom to walk directly into His presence each time you have conversation with Him.

However, like in the parable we discussed above, you must be humble and willing to walk up to Jesus' table, ask permission to take a seat, pull up your chair next to Him, and have *many* vulnerable conversations. That's how a relationship begins. Yes, the journey ahead will still be difficult. You will need to be focused and determined, so the walls don't slowly rise again. Sometimes the struggle will be difficult but God will be there when you call out and give Him full control.

That's how it happened for Tessa. When she finally realized she couldn't; she found God could. That's how relationship with God will happen for you. Hopefully, sooner than later. Unfortunately, the longer we allow the wall to remain, the more the devil has power to manipulate you and keep you stuck behind the wall.

The walls we unintentionally

erect to keep out the many

hurts we've experienced in life,

are often the same walls

that keep us from experiencing

freedom in

Jesus Christ our Lord.

CHAPTER 8

WHO KNOCKS DOWN THE WALLS

"No one can change your life but you!" How many times have you heard that phrase? Sure, we must all take steps if we desire any type of change. However, there are many struggles we are unable to accomplish alone. How do I know this? I've stood staring at the wall before me. I have asked family and friends for help and the wall didn't budge. I've gone to counseling and followed every step, only to see hairline cracks appear and fade with time. No matter how hard I worked to knock down the wall; my efforts were limited. This left me with one thought. When I can't, who can?

Maybe it was hope or maybe I was just exhausted from the struggle. Regardless, I decided to have a conversation with God. I have found the more time I spend asking God to prepare me for what's next, the more I see improvement in my life. I've never heard His audible voice. Sometimes He speaks through a scripture or impresses a thought or idea in my mind. I call this my inner voice or conscience. This time God brought back a memory.

When I was five years old, I sang in my children's church choir called the Booster Band. Imagine a small group of toddlers, preschoolers, and kindergartners, dressed in their finest with bright eyes and beaming smiles, lining up in front of the church family. When the teacher announced the next song was "The Mighty Walls of Jericho," there was a definite shift in energy. The pint-sized army stood tall with shoulders back preparing for ear-piercing volume and hand motions of exaggerated precision. Then, came the best part. We sang, "and the walls came tumbling down, boom, boom, boom," collapsing on the floor and giggling hysterically as parents applauded.

I'm no longer an innocent child and realize that the walls I've erected as an adult will be more difficult to remove than just saying, "boom, boom, boom." But the memory stirred my heart to ask myself, *what does God want me to learn or what is He speaking to my heart?*

This led me to Britannica.com to research the Walls of Jericho. They were built about 8000 BCE and measured at least thirteen feet tall in order to protect the city of Jericho and its water supply from intruders. Jericho is famous in biblical history as the first town attacked by the Israelites. Under the leadership of Joshua, God had promised specific land to the Israelites. The story begins in Joshua 5. Let me paraphrase a bit.

Joshua was out for his daily walk near Jericho. On a sunny day with few clouds in the sky, he noticed a man in the distance who appeared to have a sword. The closer he got to him the sun reflected off the blade and confirmed Joshua's assumption. He raised his voice to the man and asked, "Are you on our side, or the enemy's side?"

The man replied, "Neither, I am from the Lord's Army."

Okay, I don't know about you, but I would be wondering if I heard that right. To be honest, I wouldn't have made it close enough to hear the man's answer in the first place. But Joshua was brave and was known to have little fear when doing the Lord's work. The next thing we see reveals the very reason why God chose Joshua. He fell to his knees and bowed to the ground to show reverence for God.

Joshua had already knocked down many spiritual walls long ago that might keep him from a relationship with his God. He said, "I am your servant. Tell me what to do." The Lord's commander told him to take off his sandals because he was in a holy place. Well, you can guess what Joshua did.

Meanwhile the people of Jericho had heard "who was in town." They were afraid of the Israelites and began locking all the gates to their city.

While Joshua was placing his shoes to the side, the Lord spoke. (Joshua 6). God tells Joshua that He is giving him and the Israelites the city of Jericho. He tells Joshua and his fighting men to march around the town once a day for six days. God also tells him to take seven priests carrying ram's horns and walk in front of the Ark of the Covenant. On the seventh day, He told them to march around the city seven times, with the priests blowing their horns.

Joshua gave all the instructions to the Israelites that the Lord had given him, including telling the Israelite people to march around behind the priests and armed men and shout as loud as they could when they heard one long blast of the rams' horns. "Do not shout; do not even talk," Joshua commanded. "Not a single word from any of you until I tell you to shout. Then shout! Joshua 6:10."

"The seventh time around, as the priests sound the long blast on their horns, Joshua commanded the people, "Shout! For the Lord has given you the town!" (Joshua 6:16 NLT).

SUDDENLY THE WALLS OF JERICHO COLLAPSED

The story doesn't end there. The Walls of Jericho reveal God's redemptive plan to His people.

God first presents a gift. For the people of Israel, the gift was an abundant land that would provide, not only for their physical needs, but also a place to worship the One and only God. He instructed them in what they needed to do to receive it and then waited and watched as they followed His instructions.

When they completed everything the Lord God asked them to do, they received the promise. *The walls came tumbling down.* Just as God knocked down the massive walls enabling the Israelites to inhabit the promised land, we have walls that God will demolish as well.

In prior chapters we discussed five walls that may stand between our relationship with God: Rejection, Fear, Busyness, Perfectionism and Pride. These spiritual strongholds are difficult to knock down by you or me alone. But with God's supernatural power, great things can happen in our lives as we humble ourselves and participate in the process.

God commanded the Israelites to do two things: march and shout. Each day Joshua and the Israelites were obedient to God's instructions. They marched for approximately one hour listening to the priests blow the trumpets. On the seventh day they marched a total of seven hours. When Joshua gave the command, they began to shout as loud as they could. *I don't know about you, but I would shout for joy knowing I could finally stop marching!*

Let's look at God's Word to see what instruction He gave that causes the walls to come tumbling down. When we march (act) and shout (stand confident in praise) we will see God keep his promises to bless us for our obedience. When we ask God to knock down our emotional walls, we can apply these same scriptures to help to build our faith on the following topics.

REJECTION

March (Action): "May the God of hope fill you with all joy and peace in believing, so that by the power of the Holy Spirt you may abound in hope" (Romans 15:13 ESV).

Shout (Praise): "Joyful are people of integrity, who follow the instructions of the Lord. Joyful are those who obey his laws and search for him with all their hearts. They do not compromise with evil, and they walk only in his paths" (Psalm 119:1-3 NLT).

FEAR

March (Action): "I prayed to the Lord, and he answered me. He freed me from all my fears" (Psalm 34:4 NLT).

Shout (Praise): "I will praise the Lord at all times. I will constantly speak his praises. I will boast only in the Lord; let all who are helpless take heart" (Psalm 34:1-2 NLT).

BUSYNESS

March (Action): "Come to Me, all who are weary and carry heavy burdens (busy with cares of life), and I will give you rest. Take my yoke upon you. Let me teach you, because I am humble and gentle at heart, and you will find rest for your souls" (Matthew 11:28-29 NLT).

Shout (Praise): "…whatever you do, do all to the glory of God" (1 Corinthians 10:31 ESV).

PERFECTIONISM

March (Action): "…you are worried and upset about many things, but few things are needed or indeed only one" (Luke 10:41b-42a NLT).

Shout (Praise): "God arms me with strength, and makes my way perfect" (Psalm 18:32 NLT).

PRIDE

March (Action): "So humble yourselves before God. Resist the devil, and he will flee from you. Come close to God, and God will come close to you…" (James 4:7-8 NLT).

Shout (Praise): "Let all that I am praise the Lord; with my whole heart, I will praise his holy name. Let all that I am praise the Lord; may I never forget the good things he does for me" (Psalm 103:1-2 NLT).

When we apply God's Word to our life and are obedient to His instruction, He fights for us against the battles in our mind and wars against the anxiety, depression, and other struggles we face daily in this world. This isn't an overnight process. Remember, the wall has been erected one concrete block at a time. We must have hope and have faith to believe God's promises are true.

Belief doesn't happen overnight for most of us. Belief follows faith and hope. Let me explain. Hebrews 11:1 (NLT), says, "Faith shows the reality of what we hope for; it is the evidence of things we cannot see." Do you hope to experience the love of God in your life? Do you believe that God keeps His promises and will in time free you from your struggles?

If you can answer yes to these questions, then you have what it takes to watch God knock down your walls. With perseverance and trust in God, you will see the foundation crumble and experience God's power working in your life.

If you feel you may not have enough faith for God to do this miraculous work, let me ask you this question. Do you have even the smallest amount of faith and hope that God wants to heal your life and have an intimate relationship with you? If so, you have enough faith to begin.

Jesus told His disciples in Matthew 17:14-20, with just a tiny amount of faith the size of a mustard seed, *they could move mountains*! In this story the disciples wanted to heal a man that was demon possessed. They wondered why when they prayed the demons remained. Jesus told them it was because they didn't have enough faith. Then, he said, "I tell you the truth, if you have faith as small as a mustard seed, you can say to this mountain, 'move from here to there' and it will move; Nothing is impossible for you."

We must understand that we can only build up our own faith with God's help. With a minimal amount of trust and determination, we will see our faith grow to immense proportions because of our relationship with God. The more we pray and see God answer, the stronger we become and our faith increases.

God already has the plan. He only asks you to say hello, connect with Him through conversation, study His Word and practice what you are learning.

*In time, your desire to become like Him will increase
and your love for things in this world will decrease.*

Isn't this how all healthy relationships evolve? The more time we spend getting to know a person; the more we long to be with them. The more we commit to growing the relationship; the more our love increases. In this next chapter, we will see how God longs to 'guard our heart' and become our 'first love' from now through eternity.

When **hello** evolves into *love*

my best advice is to

depend on God's Word

to guard your heart.

Wear it like a tattoo to remind you

when other loves are fleeting;

His love is eternal.

CHAPTER 9

ONE HELLO CHANGES EVERYTHING

There is a hello that changes everything. You meet someone for the first time and during that conversation you network your way into a new job, develop a new friendship, or even meet the person that will eventually be your life-long companion. "Hello" is powerful and can lead to life-changing moments, but while here on earth these informal and formal greetings are fleeting.

That is why the hello you present to God is so powerful. This hello comes from deep inside your being. This hello, when presented with more than just a handshake or smile, comes with a desire to offer up your life to Him. This hello is eternal. Yes, with this choice to give your heart to Jesus, you are gifted by God with eternal life. No one would argue living forever isn't great. Who doesn't want to live forever?

Jesus told us that He is the RESURRECTION AND LIFE and he "who believes" WILL LIVE even if he dies (John 1125). We also know from Acts 26:18, we are set free from Satan's dominion and we receive forgiveness for our sins and receive "AN INHERITANCE…"

Eternal life is a wonderful gift. However, let's look at some benefits of a relationship with God here on earth.

> » We are *"sealed in Him (Jesus) with the Holy Spirit."* No one and nothing can separate us from God. *(Ephesians 1:13)*
> » We receive *JOY, PEACE and HOPE. (Romans 15:13)*
> » We receive *CHRIST living inside of us. (Galatians 2:20)*

» We are called *"sons of God." (Galatians 3:26)*
» We receive *boldness and confident access to God. (Ephesians 3:12)*

The list goes on! Twenty-seven times the Bible refers to "benefits" of salvation through Jesus Christ. Those are benefits that come with accepting Jesus to be your Savior. As you grow in faith, there are 788 scriptures that apply to a blessed life with Jesus as your Lord.

When you say, "Hello, God" you are claiming your inheritance. You are claiming your rights as a child of God. You are being ushered into the very presence of God. Your spirit connects with your Creator's spirit. You receive power from the Spirit of God!

Even with all the positives, it is normal for many to struggle with what we feel might be negatives to having a relationship with God. It could appear that Jesus' command that we "give up everything and follow" Him is a negative.

God is not opposed to you having things – He just doesn't want you to give them more importance or priority than your relationship with Him. Maybe you are struggling with being persecuted by others or feeling like you aren't the "real" you. Maybe you are feeling you will have to "miss out" on certain things in this life. Well, what if the world has given us the wrong view about what LIFE really is all about? Remember, scripture tells us God is love and everything He does is within the law of love!

God designed you to walk in eternal freedom. The only way this is possible is by receiving His Spirit and developing your God-given attributes. This will take a measure of patience and obedience.

God is God and He like any god, requires obedience. When we look at this same perspective through God's law of love, we see that obedience produces safety from falling into the earthly trap of sin. Sin is any deliberate action, attitude, or thought that goes against God. Sin is like a trap that sets in motion many negative consequences.

When you bring your difficult questions or situations to God and then are obedient to do what He shows you in His Word, He will continue to give you direction and help you realize when you are approaching sinful situations.

And what about persecution? Persecution comes into everyone's life whether we have a relationship with Christ or not. This planet is filled with individuals that have a spirit of persecution, which includes bullying. Unfortunately, you receive nothing for being persecuted because of your skin color, your difference in opinion, personality type, life choices, or for disabilities you may have. However, Jesus promises, *He BLESSES those who are persecuted for doing right!* (Matthew 5:10). He also promises you the Kingdom of Heaven for what you go through because of Him.

What about losing the "real" you? Well, exactly who is the "real" you? The world's version or the YOU that God created.

God creates perfectly. Yet, the minute we leave our mother's womb we experience worldly influences. We are taught things like greed, high expectations, and manipulation - all from a fallen world. So, the "real" you will not be set free to become who God created you to be unless God's Spirit lives in you and you allow Him to transform you into His likeness.

Will you miss out on things in this life? Paul wrote, "I have the right to do anything, —but not everything is beneficial" (1 Corinthians 10:23 NIV). We know in some circles that drinking a glass of wine with your meal is considered healthy. We also know that getting drunk is unhealthy and leads to negative consequences. We understand that eating fruit is healthy, but overeating apples can cause a stomach ache. We realize that exercising is healthy. However, if not done in moderation with the correct equipment and proper usage, we may hurt our physical bodies. We know that watching television can be entertaining, but excessive watching or viewing the wrong material can cause our brains to not function optimally.

Paul also pointed out, "Or do you not know that your body is a temple of the Holy Spirit within you, whom you have from God? You are not your own, for you were bought with a price. (Jesus sacrificed Himself on the cross to purchase you as His own.) So, glorify God in your body" (1 Corinthians 6:19-20).

Yes, there will be things God will advise you to remove from your life to insure health, peace, and joy. How you listen and apply God's teachings to your life is up to you. You get to choose to say hello to God and begin a relationship with Him or remain separate from Him.

Paul stated perfectly, ...*accept this marvelous gift of God's kindness and don't ignore it. For God says, "At just the right time, I heard you. On the day of salvation, I helped you." Indeed, the "right time" is now. Today is the day of salvation (2 Corinthians 6:1-2).*

My heart is racing right now. There are goosebumps lifting the hair on my arms. I'm reaching for a tissue to wipe my eyes. Why this emotion from me?

Because this "hello" you offer to the God of the universe can changes everything. When you say hello to God and make a commitment to Him, He immediately enters your Spirit and you become a new creation. You also become an heir to His throne, and a part of His family.

He tells us in His Word that when this miracle of the "new birth" occurs in your spirit, your old nature is done away with and you receive a new nature (a new spirit or core). Though your mind, will, and emotions are not immediately transformed (this is done in time by renewing your mind through scripture and trusting God), the real you will have a desire to learn more about God and grow your relationship with Him. Plus, you don't have to worry that he condemns you for your sins. He promises to throw them away and remember them no more.

God also wants you to know that when you become His child you assume your inheritance and receive the power of His Spirit. This is the same power that raised Jesus from the dead and will raise you from death to eternal life on the day of Jesus' coming. Can you believe it? *God's power inside of you!*

Maybe you are wondering what to say to God after you say hello. Although I'm not a fan of "canned" prayers, I do think a blueprint to guide you is beneficial. Architects and engineers draw blueprints to assist builders and give them a framework of what is planned. So read the following prayer but make it personal.

"God, I realize that everyone is a sinner. Though I was created by you, I was born with a sinful nature. Forgive me of all my sins. Thank you for sacrificing your life. Thank You for wiping away all my sin. Your Word says "you will remember them no more" (Hebrews 8:12). Thank you for raising Jesus up from His grave so I can one day live with you, too. Thank you for coming and making your home in my soul. Now I can learn to be more like you every day. Guide me. Love me. And, create the "real" me you intended from the beginning of the world. I ask for these things in your name, Jesus Christ, my Lord. Amen.

So, what now? That's it? That's all I need to do? Yes! You must mean what you say of course. None of this, "I'm going to build a relationship and never show up to cultivate it." That would never fly with God. *If you had a meaningful, humble conversation with God, you ARE in relationship with Him.*

What's next? Just like in any new relationship, there needs to be a lot of conversation. You must be vulnerable. The more conversations you have with God, the closer you will become to Him. If you want to hear what He has to say in return, a good place to start is reading His Word. More on that later.

I hope you are beginning to grasp the importance of not just believing there is a God, but knowing Him. Why? Because the love that God has in store for you goes beyond what we can fathom. Let's look at what occurs in relationships when you decide you have fallen deeply in love and want to take the next step.

*Let us be glad and rejoice
and give Him glory,
for the marriage of the Lamb
has come, and His wife
has made herself ready.*

Revelation 19:7

CHAPTER 10

HERE COMES THE BRIDE

Do you love weddings? Maybe you are planning your celebration or involved in the preparation with a bride-to-be. If you are, you know that no two weddings are alike. If the bride likes horses and cowboy boots, the wedding will have a western flair. If she loves elegance or is casual, you will know it as you enter the wedding venue. One common thread in all wedding celebrations: they take enormous work and planning.

Even in ancient times, wedding celebrations had a planning stage. However, before the planning could begin, the father selected the bride for his son. In the book of Genesis, Abraham instructed his servant to find a wife for his son, Isaac. Laban selected his daughter Leah for Jacob and later gave him Rachel also.

Very few women in our society would agree to their father selecting their husband. You can almost envision a picket line forming to protect the bride's rights!

In most cases, the Jewish bride would have an opportunity to decide if she was willing to accept the offer. If so, they had a ritualistic ceremony which signified they were married, but didn't consummate the marriage at that time. They lived separately until the groom's father felt everything was ready.

The groom would work hard to provide a place for he and his bride to live. He also invested in animal stock and developed his crops to plan for their future. The groom didn't know when the celebration day would be. He had to wait until his father said, "it is time." Then, he would go and get his bride. Why? Because his father made the final decision as to when he felt everything was prepared.

The bride, on the other hand, knew to expect her groom within approximately a year, but she didn't know the exact day or hour. He could come to her in the day or night. She must have her gown ready and the lamps filled with oil to be prepared. Patience and faithfulness were a must as she awaited the celebration day.

Let's look at Natalie's story. She knows firsthand the importance of being faithful and patient as she waited for a proposal from the man she loved.

Natalie

Summer had arrived. Natalie was excited to travel with Joe, her boyfriend, to Colorado to camp with Natalie's parents. On a beautiful summer day, they hiked to Natalie's favorite spot she had hiked to in prior years with her family. Everything was perfect. The perfect crystal, clear lake glittered with the sun's reflection. Beautiful wildflowers were everywhere. Natalie thought, "could this be the perfect moment?" Her expectation of Joe asking for her hand plummeted as they headed back to their campsite. Natalie was disappointed, again.

Natalie met Joe while teaching in a middle school in Oklahoma. Sitting in a staff meeting, she noticed him across the table and thought, "*oh he's cute*." Later, they saw each other in the hall and said hello. After several emails, they decided to go on a first date to the state fair. A few weeks later, Natalie received a note during class from Joe. Just like something out of a middle-school reality tv show, she opened the small handwritten note from him asking her to be his girlfriend. This started a new relationship.

Natalie was sure this was what God wanted. She had prayed for God to send her the right person and felt at peace. She also had confidence because an entire year earlier her Aunt Tammy tried to fix her up with a guy who was student teaching at the Junior High school where she worked. She never met him back then, but come to find out, Joe was the same guy.

Early in the relationship Natalie remained confident Joe was Mr. Right. She never found it difficult to make decisions and was confident she had made the right one. One Christmas she traveled to Houston to meet Joe's family. After this visit, Natalie was flying back Oklahoma alone to prepare for a planned mission trip to Africa. Joe dropped her at the airport, and it was there that they said, "I love you" for the first time. Again, this made Natalie feel she had made the right decision.

Months turned into years and Natalie realized she was more ready than Joe to get married. Any time they'd talked about the future he had put a stop to the conversation. Most of the time, Natalie was okay with this situation. She didn't want to be controlling or push Joe into making a commitment he wasn't ready for. But there were moments in her late twenties when she worried that he wasn't as serious she was, and wondered if she were wasting her time.

This wasn't the first long-term relationship Natalie had been involved in. She had felt hurt before in relationships where initially commitments were made but then ended abruptly. This caused a feeling of mistrust she couldn't ignore. She also knew her biological clock was ticking. This caused anxiety and frustration and fueled more serious discussions about the future. After five years of dating, Natalie wondered what Joe was waiting on?

She realized he was very methodical and needed not only his ducks to be in a row, but also his duck's ducks! He wanted her to realize his necessity for being prepared. He told her about his anxiety of not feeling he could take care of her on a teacher's salary. He needed more time. Natalie continued to pray and ask God if she had been right about her relationship with Joe.

A couple of months later, they headed down to Houston for another trip to visit Joe's family. Joe liked to leave around 5:30 am, so Natalie set aside her normal "getting ready" routine and rolled out of bed, hair in a messy bun, got in the car, and they were on their way. After traveling for a short time, Joe said he needed to pull over because he feared something was wrong with his tire. He yelled from behind the car for Natalie to get out and come take a look. "No, I don't have my shoes on," Natalie yelled back.

Joe was insistent and pulled her out of the car in her bare feet. He dropped down on one knee and proposed. This time, Natalie was surprised. A sense of relief washed over her. God was working things out. Not in her timing, but in His.

That was November. Natalie was excited about preparing for her wedding and wanted to set the date. "Let's get married this summer."

Again, Joe said, "slow down".

This time Natalie wouldn't have it. She said, "it's my turn; I get to decide."

So, after six years of dating, Natalie and Joe married. A lot of planning went on inside Natalie's head. She wanted to create the perfect day, not just for herself, but also for Joe. She found being a planner had benefits. Things went well as she made decision after decision and checked things off her list one by one.

When the wedding day arrived, she was excited about the ceremony. One of her favorite parts was the "first look" photo with her dad. The photographer situated her father backward so he couldn't see Natalie enter the room. "I remember walking toward my dad and telling him to turn around. He was taken aback. His eyes watered and he unsuccessfully tried to hold back tears. Men must be strong but my tears were stronger and I had to redo my makeup."

Natalie knew her dad was proud of her and all she had accomplished. The beauty of the moment made her remember how much she loved her dad. She knew he had always been the best example of Christ; he was strong, sensible, and consistent in how he loved her.

When the ceremony began, Joe was standing at the front of the room surrounded by family and friends. Joe wasn't an outwardly emotional guy, but when Natalie entered the room, his eyes began to water and a smile stretched across his face. Her white gown seemed to flow endlessly as she carried the bouquet of white roses in one hand and looped the other around her father's arm.

Natalie felt God's presence very strongly at this moment and knew God was teaching her a lesson. He had been faithful to walk beside her. Joe was faithful, too. She knew even though she'd struggled in the waiting period and wanted everything to be planned, it was patience and faithfulness that allowed her to experience the intimate love and joy of the celebration that followed.

• • •

In the Bible, God reveals his desire to have an intimate relationship with us through parables depicting the wedding ceremony. *Imagine how God reacts when we decide to choose Him.*

His heart is pounding and His face lights up, all because you chose to be His bride! The long, awaited moment becomes a reality. You chose to unite with Him in a relationship far above all others. That was the moment you made a vow to love Him with all your heart, mind, soul, and strength.

In the Bible, Jesus shared two parables or stories about wedding celebrations. In word pictures, we see the importance of being patient, being prepared, making good choices, and being faithful.

The first parable begins with Jesus saying, "The Kingdom of Heaven can be illustrated by the story of a king who prepared a great wedding feast for his son" (Matthew 22:2). The king sent his servants to invite guests to come to the wedding banquet. Yet, when his servants went to notify the guests that everything was ready, they refused to come. So, he sent more servants. Jesus went on to say they too refused to attend and "went on their way, one to his farm, and another to his business." Others were abusive by adding insults and even harming the king's servants to the point of death. What transpired next is tragic.

Just visualize the scene.

The king IS the king. What he says goes. He had a plan and was angered that he would send out such a heartfelt invite to certain people in the kingdom, yet he was turned down. He had expectations that his son would be honored on this day of all days! Think about it.

The king had tried more than once to extend the invitation. In return, the individuals put daily tasks in front of his invitation or were abusive, insulting and even committed murder. They did not show remorse or even try to make amends. Well, they got their due!

The king stated that the guests he had invited didn't deserve the honor he wanted to bestow upon them. Did the king give up? Absolutely not! He sent out the servants to bring in "anyone" that would come. Status didn't matter at this point. The invitation was open to the good and the bad – to anyone that would come. Yet, we see the invitation came with "one requirement." The guests were supposed to have on wedding clothes. This was customary for this time period. Guests were given wedding clothes from the groom's family to wear at the wedding.

It was beyond reasoning that someone would refuse the clothing offered by the groom's father. However, as the story goes on to say, there was one man that had refused the outfit given to him. When the king sees his guest not wearing the appropriate wedding attire, he addresses him. He calls out to him "friend." His choice to identify the guest as a friend reveals remorse in his tone and regret on his face. He wonders why his friend isn't dressed in the wedding clothes gifted to him.

The description Jesus gives next in this parable is heart-wrenching. The outcome of the unprepared guest is horrifying. And, the last sentence of the story weighs the heaviest on my heart.

"For many are called, but few are chosen."

If you know Jesus as I do, these words are crushing. Knowing that not everyone given an invitation to the eternal wedding will choose to participate in the celebration is weighty.

We need to remember what the king called the man whom he had never met. He called him "friend." The man had been invited to be in a relationship with the king, although the man was unwilling and silent in giving him a reason why he did not want to be a part of the wedding. He simply chose not to be prepared.

God gives His creation ample information about the need to be prepared for eternity. He offers His invitation, not just once, but time and time again. Maybe you've been given many opportunities to know Him and still are refusing His invitation. Or, maybe you know who God is yet continue to refuse to be prepared for His big celebration when He returns.

You may be thinking this is a scare tactic. No, the devil wants you to believe that is true. As a follower of Christ, I am hoping that you see the above parable and even this book as an *invitation* to eternal life with Jesus Christ. I'm hoping you know that your Creator, God the Father, is seated on the throne with Jesus and the Holy Spirit and they're *waiting to open the door and see you,* their friend, dressed and prepared to enter the wedding celebration.

Remember, the king went out of his way to do everything possible to have a relationship with friends and community. We all know that if you try to force someone into a relationship, then it's not really a relationship at all and any connection will never last.

If you flip a few pages in your Bible to Matthew, Chapter 25, you will discover another story Jesus told about a wedding celebration. This is my version.

Ten beautiful bridesmaids were all dressed up and headed to meet the bridegroom. You can almost hear their giggling, constant chatter, and undercurrent of excitement. Half of the girls were named Wise. The other half were named Foolish. There was a warm glow emitting from the lanterns each young woman carried to light their way. What a magnificent sight. Their white flowing gowns reflected their style, as did their gorgeous hair embellished with gold hairpins, flowers, and jeweled crowns. Faces were radiant, just as bridesmaids anticipating their wedding should be.

The bridesmaids reached the doors to the banquet hall. After waiting for some time, it appeared the groom was running late. Waiting is difficult for everyone but patience is needed so everything can be at its best. The young maids tried their hardest to sit still and not wrinkle their gowns or dishevel their hair that took hours to set. One brave girl inquired as to what was keeping the groom. Unfortunately, she wasn't given any reasons for the delay.

Eyes close and heads droop as the bridesmaids resign themselves to take a needed catnap. While they were sleeping, the oil in their lamps burned low. "No need for alarm," said one of the maids from the Wise family. We brought extra oil for our lamps.

"Would you be willing to share some of your oil with us?" asked a maid from the Foolish family.

I imagine the Foolish maids had observed the others had brought extra oil with them. Like some people you may know, they are never prepared and have a pattern of depending on others to dig them out of their problems. Don't get me wrong, I am the first to help a friend in need. However, Jesus was trying to drive a point home in this parable. What happened next? Jesus' point became clear.

"I'm so sorry. If we share our oil with you, we will run out and no one will be prepared," voiced another Wise maid, "but you could go back into town and purchase more oil."

The point here is that being prepared for the coming of the groom should be our highest priority. All the bridesmaids had the same amount of time and access to be ready but only half planned and followed through for the big event.

Not long after the Foolish bridesmaids had headed off to town, there was a slight rattle of the doorknob. The Wise bridesmaids began checking their makeup in the mirror, making last-minute adjustments to their hairdos, and making sure their gowns were flowing just right.

The five Wise maidens stood in their positions as the huge double doors slowly opened before their eyes. There standing in all his glory, the groom smiled from ear-to-ear and ushered the bridesmaids into the marriage feast.

Observe something important regarding these bridesmaids. He didn't say the most beautiful were the only ones that could enter. He didn't say the smartest, the strongest, or the richest either. What did He say? It was the wise. Wise in this scripture is placed opposite foolish. It can't be compared to GPA or your IQ. The definition for wise is "showing experience, knowledge and good judgment."

These characteristics are not ones you are generally born with; they are learned. This means that no one is exempt. It is our responsibility to learn and use our sound judgment in deciding to have a relationship with Jesus.

Jesus says that God has given you everything you need to accept Him as Lord of your life. He does not make exceptions for those who are unwise and refuse His invitation. Then, if you read what happens in verse 10, your stomach may feel a bit queasy.

"He locked the door!"

The finality of this is no joke! Jesus goes on to say that when the Foolish brides returned and knocked on the door, the groom only yelled to them from the inside. Does this seem cruel? Can you picture the Foolish bridesmaids dropping their heads low? Maybe some even cried out in agony as tears fell from their eyes. The story doesn't end there. The groom raised his voice and spoke one of the most painful statements to bear. He said, *"I don't know you."*

Then like in every parable, the truth behind the story is revealed. In verse 13 he gives advice to all who will hear. Jesus went on to say, *"YOU must keep watch!"*

This statement then makes you wonder the why? "For you do not know the day or hour of my return."

Okay, so at this point you either build up your towers of pride or fall to the floor in humble abandonment. The message is clear. He is coming. We don't know when, but it will happen.

Again, this is no scare tactic. This is just the TRUTH and the IRREVOCABLE plan of God. Nothing significant you ever accomplish in your life comes into fruition without planning, hard work, and consistency. This holds true when developing a relationship with your Creator. This has been the plan from the beginning. Create and bring all men into relationship with God.

Please don't discard this book and ignore its message. Please dig deep and resolve for yourself the importance of this conversation. This parable is for everyone. When Jesus comes as the bridegroom, everyone that is prepared is like the bride.

I don't like the "fire and brimstone" or "condemnation" message. I never have. I doubt you do either. So, look with me at this depiction of the same story.

You are one of the wise brides. You get up early every day anticipating the moment your bridegroom (Jesus) will be waiting for you. You study every wedding detail from books online and ones you've purchased from the store. You search God's Word for any information to help you prepare.

You learn all you can about the groom in order to please Him and fulfill His heart's desire. You prepare yourself outwardly of course. Find just the right wedding attire. You are patient. This is a must because the groom has also been working hard to prepare the festivities for you.

> *Then it happens! You hear the voice of*
> *the groom saying, "All is ready!"*

The music begins to play and the door opens wide. There is an unmistakable glow, an uncontainable feeling that surges through the veins of all those attending the celebration. Why? Because this is the moment when everyone will be united! This is the moment you have longed for ever since you humbly asked Jesus to come into your heart and be a part of your life. This is when the God of the universe will be one with you. Then it happens! Across the room, you see Him. You see His face! You are "perfected." You become like Him.

Jesus told us, "And if I go and prepare a place for you, I will come back and take you to be with me that you may also be where I am" (John 14:3 NLT). Jesus invites you to be His bride. Yes, especially YOU. Your family and friends, too. Yes, even the men in your life are called to be the BRIDE of Christ.

Tim Keller, a well-known Christian author wrote, "Men, you'll never be a good groom to your wife, unless you're FIRST a good bride to Jesus."[10]

Uniting with someone in marriage is the beginning of potentially the greatest relationship you can have with someone. There is no greater depiction of faithfulness and love that Jesus could have given than the wedding ceremony. And He, the Creator of the universe, the One that created YOU, wants to join with you forever in the greatest love story of all.

Oh, the amount of emotion that Jesus longs for you to experience in this moment. He created you, He came to earth and died for you. Now, He prepares a place for you to spend eternity with Him. He has planned every detail of the celebration. He has invited everyone and you're included. An account of what this moment will be like is found in the book of Revelation 19:6-10.

Then I heard again what sounded like
the shout of a vast crowd or the roar of mighty oceans
waves or the crash of loud thunder. "Praise the Lord!
For the Lord our God, the Almighty, reigns.
Let us be glad and rejoice, And let us give honor to him.
For the time has come for the wedding feast of the Lamb,
And his bride has prepared herself.
She has been given the finest of pure white linen to wear."
For the fine linen represents the good deeds
of God's holy people.
And the angel said to me, "Write this: Blessed are those
who are invited to the wedding feast of the Lamb."
And he added, "These are true words that come from God."

There is an expectation here. There is something that needs to be done. No, we don't have to purchase wedding attire. Jesus already provides everything. All we need to do is accept His invitation, choose to build a relationship with Him, and be humble to give Him control of your life. Jesus says in Revelations 22:12,

> *"Look, I am coming soon! My reward is with me,*
> *and I will give to each person according*
> *to what they have done."*

Remember the wise virgins waiting for the groom? They were waiting with expectancy. They were focused and prepared when they heard the rattle of the doorknob. They didn't give up. He made it clear that everyone will not be recognized as someone He knows. He is not excluding. He has set up eternal boundaries which only allow Him to enter the life of those that invite Him in. Because of choice, He forces no one to be in relationship with Him.

He has a reward for those who "know" Him. This is not just a head knowledge experience. This word "know" conveys the highest level of intimacy.

Just like Natalie became Joe's bride, they both are the bride of Christ. You can also be one of His brides! Jesus wants you to set aside all your earthly desires and prideful attitudes and say, "I am yours!" This means that Jesus wants you to take Him along through the good and the bad, through the ups and downs, through feelings of uncertainty, even doubt. Jesus wants a deep, raw, and forever binding relationship with You. This is what He has wanted from the beginning when the world was first created.

Relationship, relationship, relationship.

What more can anyone ask for than to be in relationship with the God of the universe? Everything else seems pale against this! Can money be greater, can fame? Can earthy relationships that are filled with so much frailty? NO! Nothing is greater than the love of Jesus in you!

I couldn't say it better than this…

"The Lord your God is with you, he is mighty to save.
He will take great delight in you,
he will quiet you with his love,
he will rejoice over you with singing."
Zephaniah 3:17

Picture this: God is surrounding you with so much love that regardless of what wall stands in the way He will demolish it and save you. He will knock down and destroy anything that stands in the way if you cry out for His help. He will clear a path for you to follow. He will gather you up in His arms and pull you close. He will delight in the very presence of you! He will quiet your fears with His love. And then, just like a mother sings a lullaby to her baby, He will sing over you!

The very moment you choose Jesus as the Lord of your life, the relationship is sealed. In a beautiful depiction of two lovers, Solomon wrote, "Place me like a seal over your heart, like a seal on your arm; for love is as strong as death, it's jealousy unyielding as the grave. It burns like blazing fire like a mighty flame" (Song of Solomon 8:6).

Nothing is stronger than the love Jesus has for you. It can never be destroyed and nothing can keep it from you, not even death.

So now, let me ask you a question? If Jesus were here at the table and asking you to be his bride, would you say "Yes?"

Did I hear right? Is that a resounding, YES!

That is the word Jesus has been waiting to hear since God drafted the first blueprint of you. He wants to be in a one-on-one relationship. He wants to enter your soul and reside in your spirit so you can have a relationship with Him.

Do you feel in your heart He is calling you? I have done my best to introduce you to Jesus in such a way that you understand His purpose for creating you was for relationship. I hope my words have expressed the enormous feeling of love I feel for God. If so, my work is complete.

Maybe when you opened this book, you began to identify with experiences like my friends have shared. Maybe you have always assumed you had a relationship with God, but you have recognized walls that keep you from a deeper fellowship with Him. Maybe you have decided your relationship with God is nothing more than a "religious experience." Guess what?

God does not see our past as defining us;
only preparing us.

His Word says to leave behind the past and start new today. As you read the verses below, fill in the blanks with your name.

"This is how much God loved _______________: He gave his son, his one and only son, so that when _________________ believes in him, she will not perish but have eternal life."
(John 3:15 paraphrased. for emphasis).

"If_________________declares with her mouth, "Jesus is Lord," and believes in her heart that God raised Jesus from the dead, she will be saved. For it is with your heart that you believe and are justified (made right with God), and it is with your mouth that you profess your faith and are saved."
Romans 10:9-10 (paraphrased for emphasis).

If you can identify with these verses, God longs to forgive you of all your sins. When you believe God raised Jesus from the dead and make Him the Lord of your life, He saves you and gifts you with eternal life. He takes your past and throws it from His sight to be remembered no more. Then, He creates in you a clean spirit and begins transforming you into a new creation. (2 Corinthians 5:17).

I'm hoping you have already made the decision to say "hello" and begin your life with Him. If not, the next chapter may help you with your unsure feelings.

Want a **relationship** with Jesus?
You must be willing to let go

of the big "I"

and allow **Him to be first**

in your life.

This isn't a one-time thing

--this is a daily process.

CHAPTER 11

STILL UNSURE

Are you the type of person that finds making decisions an overwhelming, difficult duty of life? You have been making decisions all your life, but you still have anxiety wondering if you are making the right choice. God created you with critical thinking skills. Experience tells us that some are more gifted in this area than others. Yet, the result of decision-making is true for all of us. Choices steer us down the path toward the future.

From this perspective alone, you can easily see how accepting Christ as Lord of your life is an extremely important one. In fact, this decision is the most important decision you will ever make in your life. Why? Because if your decision is NOT to follow Christ, then you have still decided. In this decision you are for Him or against Him. There is not a middle ground.

Wait, what if I am not against Him but just don't want to make the decision right now? Well, postponing is still deciding. So, my question to you is, "What is the underlying motive or reason behind NOT making Jesus Lord of your life."

Which walls are you allowing to stand between you and God? Is it rejection, fear, busyness, perfectionism, or pride? Maybe you have a different wall than one of these standing in your way.

Whatever strongholds are keeping you from seeing Jesus face-to-face, keeping you from receiving your eternal inheritance, or keeping you from experiencing blessings on this journey here on earth that God intended for you, then is your choice to continue to stay separated from God worth it?

I realize that because God is a spiritual being, you may find it difficult to see that you can have a genuine, personal relationship with Him. Yet, in His Word, He clearly shows us that "relationship" is the key that opens the door. Imagine this….

Jesus walks into the coffee shop. He looks around and sees you and I sitting at a table by a window. He sees the steam rising from our cups and notices we are in deep conversation. A conversation about Him. (Yes, He is God, so He is omniscient and knows everything, right?) He heads for the counter and orders His favorite cup of brew and then casually heads in our direction. I don't instantly recognize Him, but He recognizes me. He calls me by name. My heart quickens. I look deep into His eyes and realize who He is. He politely asks if He can sit with us and pulls out the empty chair next to you. Peering into His cup, He asks this question and calls you by name.

(Fill your name in the blank)

"_____________________, do you love me?" You respond, "Who are you that I should love you?" There is a pause as He looks in my direction and asks a question, "Darla, who do you say I am?"

I immediately respond, "You are the Christ, Son of the Living God." We each take a sip of our coffee and keep our eyes on the cup.

Jesus again, looks in your direction and asks, "_______________, do you love me?"

I see tears pooling in your eyes. I offer you a napkin to catch them as they glide down your cheeks. "Yes, Lord, I love you."

Can you picture yourself in this scenario? Is your heart humbled? Have you paused one of the numerous times in the book to invite Jesus into your life?

If you have, then the words Jesus spoke below will help you along your journey.

Jesus tells us that our priority should be to love Him! You can't get stronger, more powerful words than "love the Lord your God with

ALL your heart." Then He goes on to drive home the point by saying "with all your soul and mind." Covering all the parts of the human body that deal with relationship, He even adds "your strength" to the equation (Mark 12:30).

So, I must ask you. Is there still a wall standing in your way? Is it because you don't understand the urgency? Is it because of pride and your belief that your way is better? Is it because you don't quite get the reason why you should have a relationship with God?

Several reasons exist why a person doesn't choose to have a relationship with God. Most times it just boils down to absence of knowledge or unbelief. These are both choices, too.

Let's look at a good example of this in Mark 6:1-6 NLT. Jesus was in His hometown and was found teaching in the synagogue. Everyone there was amazed at how much wisdom and power He had, even to perform miracles. Though they were amazed, they began to whisper, "He's just a carpenter, the son of Mary and the brother of James, Judas, Joseph and Simon. And His sisters live right here among us!" The tone gave a sense that they were deeply offended and they refused to believe that what He was teaching came from God. Jesus' words that came next were surely ones of a broken heart. These were His relatives, friends, neighbors and even His immediate family! The very people He grew up with, knew from school, and went to the temple with.

Jesus remarked, "A prophet is honored everywhere except in his own hometown and among his relatives and his own family."

The scripture goes on to say that He was only able to heal a few sick people because of the unbelief that filled the place. So, He left Nazareth. He went from village to village and did great miracles everywhere except in His own town. Do you see? Because the people didn't believe, Jesus was unable to bless them or perform miracles for them.

Having a relationship with God and experiencing His power in your life is a CHOICE.

This is heartbreaking for God. He gave you a free will, hoping you would choose to love Him, yet many people choose other things instead of Him. You are given opportunity after opportunity to get to know Him and still you refuse. You CHOOSE your own desires over the desires of your heavenly Father. But God keeps loving and keeps on reaching to touch your heart and draw you to Himself.

I know how heartbreaking it can be to allow my children freedom to make their own choices, especially when you know the pain some of those choices can cause. Without choice, there is no authentic love. But choice fueled with pride causes all kinds of problems in our life, even among those searching for God. That is why when making choices, we should check the motives behind our decisions. Pride tells you that you have been quite capable of caring for yourself this long, so why choose God now?

Tracy Dickens, Psychologist, explains it to us like this, "Pride causes turmoil because we focus on the fruit, not the root. We shift our focus from God to self; centering our attention on the created and ignoring the Creator."[11]

When we focus our attention on God, the relationship grows stronger and our life aligns with His perfect plan. In the same way when we ignore our Creator, these negative identifiers are evident.

» Constantly Frustrated

God created you to walk in a perfect plan that He designed specifically for you. The plan takes into consideration your many gifts, passions, and attributes (Hebrews 13:21 NLT). Choosing a plan that is outside God's will for your life will eventually leave you with regret and burnout. God has your best interest at heart and wants to bring you peace as you trust your life to Him (Jeremiah 29:11 NLT).

» You may feel there is little to show for your effort.

Jesus wants us to work hard in whatever we do "as if we were doing it for the Lord." (Colossians 3:22). If we are doing it for our own gain, we will become worn out with little to show for our effort. If God is not in communication with us on a regular basis, we can get off track and go in circles.

» You are exhausted and long for rest.
Spending time with God is how we find rest and calm for our soul. The book of Hebrews tells us, "So we see that because of their unbelief they were not able to enter his rest" (Hebrews 3:19). Having a relationship with God is where He will begin to teach you how to find this rest. Jesus said, "Take my yoke upon you. Let me teach you, because I am humble and gentle at heart, and you will find rest for your souls" (Matthew 11:29 NLT).

*You may feel a constant longing to
search for the next big thing.*

Nothing in this life really can satisfy for long because you have never "let go" of your own thinking and given "all" areas of your life to following Jesus. You continue to search for the thing that you were created to discover, not realizing Jesus is the only answer. Unfortunately, without relationship with God, your perfect plan will never transpire. So, you keep searching.

*Pride can only be overcome when you decide
Jesus is first above everything in your life!*

I love the story documented in Luke 7:36-38, 44-48 (NLT). Jesus was invited to dinner at one of the Pharisees' homes, so He went. When Jesus sat down to eat, a woman that was considered quite immoral brought a beautiful alabaster jar filled with expensive perfume to Jesus. There on the dirty floor with her face looking at Jesus' dusty feet, she began to weep. It was obvious that her heart was overwhelmed with love for the one that had made a difference, not only in her life, but the lives of others she had met along the way.

The story goes on to say that as her tears fell on his feet, she began to dry them with her hair. Then she kissed his feet and applied perfume to them. Simon, who had witnessed this act, was appalled that the woman used expensive perfume to wash Jesus' feet. He felt the perfume should have been sold and the money donated to help the poor. Jesus called out his prideful attitude.

You see, Simon thought his way was better. But Jesus praised the humble attitude of this woman over His dearest disciple.

He then said, "I tell you, her sins, and they are many, have been forgiven, so she has shown me so much love..." Then He looked directly at the woman and said, "Your sins are forgiven."

The point? Though this woman had not yet received forgiveness for her sins, she was giving what she had to be in relationship with Jesus. She humbled herself at the feet of Jesus and gave *her best* to acknowledge that He was the most important person in her life. She chose Him.

> *In order to have relationship with Jesus,*
> *you must be willing to let go of the big "I" and*
> *allow Him to be first in your life.*
> *This isn't a one-time thing--this is a daily process.*

So, now is the time to be honest with yourself and accept that God is calling you to join with Him. I encourage you to accept your position as heir in His kingdom. How this will play out in your life is totally up to you. The testimonies of other believers that have gone before you are all diverse. This would make sense as we are all created differently in one aspect or another. So, for me to tell you exactly how this will transpire would be ludicrous. Your relationship is between you and God. If you are asking me where to go from here or helpful hints to get started, I would be happy to share what I have experienced and what I've learned from His Word.

My relationship has literally been all over the place with God. As I shared earlier, just like David, I started out loving God as young child, then as an adult pridefully choosing to turn away from His plan for my life. There have been moments when He has taken me by the shirt and shook the foolishness right out of me in order to get my attention. And, then there have been moments when I was down on myself from past choices and He gently led me to places in His Word to encourage me.

There have also been moments where He directed me to Scripture to allow me to see my thinking was off base. Never have I felt *condemned or without hope* in Him. Yes, there have been moments when I was unsure, steeped in fear from the uncertainties in life, and doubted His plan. BUT (this is the kind of "but" I love), *He has never left me, turned His back on me, or made me feel anything other than being His dearly loved child.*

When I keep my mind on Him, His powerful, never-ending, all-encompassing love overwhelms me from my head to my toes. And without a doubt I know you can experience the same thing.

"Jesus Christ is the same yesterday, today and forever"
(Hebrews 13:8 NLT).

This means that He loved you on the first day you were a thought in His mind and years ago when you made choices of which you are not proud. He loves you today when you ask Him to be your Lord and continues until the day you take your last breath. Always remember, God IS love.

Advice is only effective when you receive it and practice it;
the change is then manifested in your heart,
mind, soul, and strength.

If I can offer any advice that I am POSITIVE will bring life-changing results, this is it. Wait for it…

LOVE GOD

» Love Him with all your feelings (heart). That means to share all your excitement and your sadness with Him. Tell him about your fears and your hopes.

» Love Him with all your spiritual worship (soul). Praise Him for being your God. Be thankful from the depths of your being for LIFE that is abundant.

» Love Him with all your mind (thinking). Study His Word, think about what He means to you, and ponder Him in the quiet moments you spend alone with Him.

» Love Him with all your strength (service). Give Him whatever you have been given and serve others with your time, remembering the second commandment to "love one another as He has loved you."

This is the expectation of God's heart.

He wants YOU! He wants to share His love with you! He wants to pour out blessings on you! He wants to sing over you, hold you, gather you up in His arms and just be with you!

I may never meet you on the street, in my neighborhood, at my doctor's office or in line at a grocery store. I may never get a chance to have a face-to-face conversation with you or know if you have taken this opportunity to start a relationship with Jesus.

Yet, the moment you accept Jesus' invitation to be a part of His eternal plan for your life, you will have the assurance of meeting the rest of His family at the Marriage Celebration that He is preparing for us when He returns.

The girls whose stories you have read in this book want you to know they hope to see you there, too. This is how I see it transpiring…

When we arrive in heaven, we will find the perfect coffee shop. We will have our favorite cup of coffee or maybe a chai latte. We will have a moving conversation about the day you chose this book off the shelf. You will share your story of how you found an intimate spot all by yourself and opened the cover. You will tell me you found it hard to put it down (wink) until the last word was read. (Yes, I'm laughing).

We will hug each other (no more masks, sickness, or pain, etc.) and even jump up and down when you get to the part where you invited Jesus to be the Lord of your life. We will sit and wait patiently for Jesus to join us at the table. While we are waiting, we look around the room and see our relatives and friends that arrived before us.

Then the door opens and Jesus enters the room. He walks right over to our table and He calls you by name. He speaks in a voice that silences the crowd. While looking deep into your eyes, His voice resonates these words…

WELL DONE, MY GOOD AND FAITHFUL SERVANT!

Then we will party! And, oh what a party that will be! That day is coming. I can't wait. I would like to leave you with these words on the next page from your Lord and Savior, Jesus Christ.

"Don't let your **hearts** be troubled.

Trust God, and trust also in me.

There is enough room in my **Father's** home.

If this were not so, would I have told you

that I am going to prepare a place for you?

When everything is ready,

I will come and get you,

so that you will always be with me where I am.

And you know the way to where I am going."

John 14:1-4 NLT

MY FINAL THOUGHTS

I love saying hello. Goodbye not so much. As I type these final words, I am hoping you've experienced the love of God on this journey. The road ahead won't always be easy. As you travel through the rubble of your past, you must be intentional with your conversations with Jesus. He will be with you each step of the way.

If you are just starting a relationship with God and worry about what's next, I have another area of this book just for you. If you already have a relationship with God, but are not quite sure where you are in that relationship, you may also find some of the information helpful.

Steps to Develop an Intimate Relationship with God will help you on your journey. You will learn how to have intimate conversations with God, about dreams and visions, where to find support and other helpful tips for developing your relationship with your Creator.

I hope you enjoyed our journey together. I will look forward to the day we meet Jesus and sit down together, enjoying a cup of coffee with all my dear friends introduced to you in this book. Many blessings on your new journey!

Darla Czeropski

Steps to Develop an Intimate Relationship with God

The three basic areas to focus on when building an intimate, healthy relationship with God are: *conversation, support, and continued growth.* You may want to take one week for each topic to give you time to apply what you learn. Or, you may want to work through the entire study and then return to the areas where you feel need more attention. I believe whichever you choose, God will bless you for your effort. Remember, God rewards those who diligently search for Him. (Hebrews. 11:6).

INTIMATE CONVERSATION

Conversation with God is the number one way to develop your relationship with Him. Before God's Word was in print, Adam and Eve walked and talked with God in the Garden. Moses walked on a mountain and God spoke to him through a burning bush. Samuel heard God's voice while lying in bed. These moments can be found in the Bible from Genesis to 1 Samuel. This method of communicating by talking directly to Him is what God planned for us, too.

Intimate conversation with God is different than praying recited prayers. There are no set rules when talking to God. *He allows you to be real and tell it as you feel.* He doesn't judge you. You don't need fancy words or repetitious written prayers. The more time you spend with God, the more you will notice your prayers changing. You may recall and share with Him scripture you've memorized in His Word. This will build your faith as you are reminded of what He promised.

Prayer is communicative, contemplative, or even silent. All are ways we communicate with God. I prefer communicative, but am working on being more still and silent to hear from God. You can talk to God in your mind or speak to Him out loud. Sometimes my conversation with God is vocal; other times it's quiet. I talk to Him and ask questions about my feelings. I also ask Him to prepare me for what is next in my life. Sharing about our concerns, needs, and even wants is exactly what He tells us to do in His Word. "Don't worry about anything; instead, pray about everything. Tell God what you need, and thank him for what he has done" (Philippians 4:6 NLT).

Then, I pause to listen. Sometimes I hear Him speaking in my mind. I write down what He impresses on me in my journal. Then, looking for scripture that applies to the topic I'm praying about can confirm that what I am thinking aligns with what I feel He is saying to me. Sometimes, I'm led to other scriptures to reinforce or redirect my path.

I also talk to God about family and friends; asking Him for direction, protection, and to bless their lives. Asking Him to direct me in ways I can serve others is one way I can follow His greatest commandments to love my neighbor. (Matthew 22:39 NLT)

When I need an answer, I have a three-point rule. If I feel He is directing me to do something specific I wait for confirmation. Sometimes confirmation comes within the message from a minister as he speaks, sometimes from a family member, and other times from conversations with a close friend or trusted mentor. When I have confirmed the answers align with scripture, I take steps forward.

When the first confirmation comes my way, I take note and keep watch for others that may follow. When the second arrives, I write it down in my journal, continue to pray and ask God for guidance. When the third is confirmed, I feel it is a green light to move forward.

How God speaks is up to Him. Patience is needed because the wait may sometimes be lengthy. I know in these times He is working everything out for His purpose and will. Working everything for my good (Romans 8:28 NLT).

I talk to God in the morning and spend time reading a devotion. I ask Him to apply what I've read to my life. I talk to God in the car, while I'm doing household chores, when I take a walk, or even silently in my thoughts as I go throughout my day. Sometimes, I just whisper or even shout (wink), "Help me" when I don't know what to do.

If you were raised praying written prayers, you can continue to pray this way. However, I feel every relationship grows through intimate, personal conversation. God created you with a sensitive soul, creative heart, and intelligent mind to develop and use for His glory. Through personal conversations you have with Him, you will become more like Him. Share your deepest feelings and concerns with God and you will bond with Him at a deeper level.

This is a personal act of worship to God and must be just that. You should develop your own system for praying to God and hearing from Him. God's only instruction regarding prayer is to walk into His presence humbly when we come to Him to pray. Jesus then takes our words and presents them to God our Heavenly Father. Romans 8:26 says, *"In the same way, the Spirit helps us in our weakness. We do not know what we ought to pray, but the Spirit himself intercedes for us……"*

He then searches our heart and knows our mind and prays to God for us within God's will (Romans 8:27 Paraphrased).

In the space below, use the bolded guide words to write a personal conversation with God.

PRAISE HIM (Be thankful)

HUMBLY ASK GOD'S FORGIVENESS

(Be sorry for past mistakes, thoughts you need help controlling,
feelings you would like Him to transform or actions
you know would not have pleased Him)

MAKE YOUR REQUESTS KNOWN

(Yes! God wants you to ask for ALL your needs)

THANK HIM IN ADVANCE

(Always be thankful and anticipate answers to prayer)

DREAMS AND VISIONS

God can also speak through dreams and visions. God came to Abram in a vision (Genesis 15:1), appeared to Joseph in a dream (Genesis 28), and came to Job in a whirlwind (Job 38). He spoke to Moses in the Book of Exodus from within a burning bush and to Gideon in a dream (Judges 7). In the New Testament, He came to Paul in a vision in the night (Acts 16).

Dreams and visions are one way God can speak to His people. How God speaks to you will be revealed as you surrender your life to Him. Your motives to hear from God must be pure. You must want His will in all areas of your life for Him to reveal Himself to you and give you direction. These revelations may be difficult to discern (know) when you are a new Christian, but will become clearer the more time you spend with God. Pray for God to give you wisdom and ask for spiritual counsel from several trusted believers to determine and confirm everything aligns or agrees with scripture.

Since God often speaks to us through our minds, a great place to start is asking Him to renew your thoughts. His healing power is available to relieve and even remove anxiety, fear, and doubt that has built up over years of living on the earth.

The Apostle Paul taught "Do not conform to the pattern of this world, but be transformed by the renewing of your mind. Then you will be able to test and approve what God's will is – His good, pleasing and perfect will" (Romans 12:2).

I suggest you get a journal and a Bible. Hard or soft back Bibles can be found for purchase at bookstores or online. You can also download a free Bible app on a cell phone. Accessing the Bible from your cell phone is convenient and there are many translations, too. I prefer NIV or NLT. Find one that works best for you.

Journal your conversations with God. This will allow you to go back and see the prayers you have asked and those God answers. I can promise you this -- He always answers when you call out to Him. Sometimes it's a YES, sometimes a NO, and many times it will be WAIT. God is always working for your best interest and His timing is perfect. I enjoy writing down my requests in my prayer journal. This way I can refer to them at the end of the year and see how God is answering my prayers.

Look up the following scripture. Pray and ask God for insight. Write in your journal or use the space provided to write what these scriptures mean to you.

Isaiah 30:21

1 John 5:14

Read God's Word

Reading God's Word is the most active way God will speak to you. Scripture is very similar to reading a road map. It's God's direction for our lives. In the Bible, there are many examples of individuals who had a problem and how God was there to solve it. There are commandments, instructions, and promises presented throughout the Bible to make our lives fruitful and powerful.

When you find a scripture that speaks directly to you in the place you are struggling within your life, write it down. Ask God to give you knowledge and understanding as to what you need to learn from His Word. You can choose from numerous Bible studies to encourage and give you viewpoints to learn more about God. You can find these for free online and join a women's interactive Bible study that coincides with your station in life.

If you are not sure where to begin reading in the Bible, I would start with the book of Psalms or the gospel of John. Remember, God's Word is a love letter to you. Soak it up, cherish those words, and know that God will transform your heart, mind, soul, and even at times your physical body.

As you journal your conversations with God, also journal your thoughts about devotions or scriptures you are reading. You can memorize scripture and apply it to your life as well. There is tried and true evidence that reciting and applying scripture is life-changing. I love to write the scriptures on 3x5 index cards and place them strategically in my home, car, and in my workplace to find encouragement or help me memorize God's Word throughout the day.

The more you read God's Word, the more you will be able to understand God's will for your life. His true and perfect will.

Look up the following scriptures. Pray and ask God for insight. Write in your journal or use the space provided to write what this scripture means to you.

John 8:31-32

WHERE CAN I FIND SUPPORT IN MY WALK WITH GOD?

Connect with a Mentor

Fellowship or living life with other believers is extremely important. Finding individuals who are like-minded in their faith is empowering. They can study with you, pray for you, and be accountability partners regarding your faith and love for Jesus. If you are not ready for a church community because you are nervous about attending alone, maybe ask a friend you know who attends church if you could visit with them. Or, you could call a nearby Christian church and ask if they have mentors. These are individuals who will help you with the first steps and walk beside you to grow your relationship with Christ.

Mentors are not counselors or therapists. Counselors and therapists are licensed individuals who work with you to determine the best way to reach preferred outcomes in life. They help you set goals to heal from past traumas you may still be struggling with today. They have studied in their field of expertise to find the most effective path to develop disciplines concerning a person's mental health and well-being.

Mentors are partners with Christ; friends in the Christian faith to help you learn more about Jesus and His will. Mentors may share personal experiences but should direct you to the Bible for answers. The first role of a mentor is through friendship and education. They should provide accountability regarding Jesus' mission. They also will be available to help during times of need both spiritually and physically by offering support. When tragedy strikes or in times of emotional stress, your mentor can help connect you with a church community or even help you locate a professional that can be of tremendous help.

A word of advice: always ask God for guidance in this area. Take your time. Remember Christian or not, we are human, and not everyone who says they are a Christian can truthfully claim that distinction. Look for individuals who have wholesome behavior, refrain from gossip, treat others kindly, and practice self-control. Ask for referrals from a church you may consider visiting near you. If you are diligent in finding a loving and supportive mentor, God will direct you to the right place.

Look up the following scriptures. Pray and ask God for insight. Write in your journal or use the space provided to write what these scriptures mean to you.

Proverbs 27:17

Ecclesiastes 4:9-10

Connect with a Church Community

The internet has made this easy. You can find most churches online by searching churches in your area. Many churches have their services "live" online. You can participate in their worship service and hear ministers from the comfort of your home before you attend in person.

It is important to know the "church" is not just a building. The church is the people. People set up how the church is going to lead their congregation based on their purpose and vision. What a church believes and their vision should be on the church website. These should be marked by scripture to identify what God has called them to focus on as part of their mission. My church's purpose is to "Love God and Love People" which is notated with scripture in Matthew 22:36-40. Everything they do within the church is guided by that statement. Their mission is found in Matthew 28:19 which instructs us to "Go and make disciples...."

If you decide to visit a church, make sure you are familiar with what they believe. There are many denominations. Research and see if the one you decide to visit aligns with what you believe and what scripture states as truth. See if they offer programs to encourage growth and deepen your walk with Christ. I use the rule of three. Visit three or more Sundays before you make a commitment. Ask to visit with a minister in the church before you commit. They can answer any questions you have regarding the church. *The place you choose to worship is a wonderful place to learn about Jesus and meet those who want to grow in their relationship with Him.*

Look up the following scriptures. Pray and ask God for insight. Write in your journal or use the space provided to write what these scriptures mean to you.

Hebrews 10:24-25

Colossians 3:16

Connect with a Small Group

When you decide on a church family, I would suggest you also begin to look for a small group within the church community if available. Most churches have a wide selection of small groups based on whether you are male or female, your age, marital status, and even activities you love. For instance, my church has Sisterhood groups which range from Women College Students, Mom's & Tots, Golf, Christian Book Studies and Crafters. If your church is not able to provide a group specifically for you, I would ask a friend to guide you to a Christian group in your community or research Christian meet-ups in your area. Why is this so important? For several reasons, which include:

» It's a place where you are valued and become part of an extended family.
Christian relationships are important to every believer. When life is hard, they will support you and stand by you through your rough season. When you want to celebrate, they will be cheering you on.

» They give you an opportunity to grow in leadership, develop communication skills, and learn to serve.
During small group times, you can ask questions or share about your experiences. As you grow in the Lord, you may feel called to lead a small group. By connecting with another leader or the person in charge of small groups at your church, you will be directed in steps to become a leader if that is your desire. There may also be opportunities to serve with your small group in the church or surrounding community.

» They will provide individual support, Godly advice, encouragement, and accountability.
As you develop relationships with your small group leader and members of your group, you may need individual support in

areas of accountability or spiritual growth. Your group can give you godly advice and help with accountability by reaching out to you during the times between studies. They can pray for you, call you, and text you to offer support.

» You will gain wisdom and knowledge through studying the Word of God.
One of the most vital parts of a small group Bible study is their ability to spend several weeks on one subject as you study God's Word and take time to apply what you've learned. Small groups may study topics to help you in areas where you struggle and teach you how to apply God's Word to your day-to-day life.

Small groups exist so you can engage in biblical community and grow in your relationship with Jesus.

WHAT MORE CAN HELP ME GROW IN MY RELATIONSHIP WITH GOD?

Baptism

Were you baptized as a baby? Water baptism looks different as an adult. In this baptism, you're following the example of Jesus. You've made a mature decision to follow and commit to be a disciple of Jesus Christ. Water submersion is an outward expression of your commitment to God. Think of it as a testimony or visual representation of preaching the Gospel. When you stand in the water you are symbolizing dying on the cross. Being immersed in the water symbolizes being buried in the tomb. The moment you rise out of the water symbolizes being risen from the dead. You bury your old life and step into a new life.

You can find an example of water baptism in Mark 3:21. Jesus was baptized in the Jordan River as an example for us to follow. This doesn't mean you have to be baptized in the Jordan River. (Ha!) There are many places you can be baptized.

You can find a church to assist you. Most churches have baptismal pools and even instruction to help you have better understanding of what the Bible says about baptism. You can also have a Christian friend assist you in your baptism in a pool or lake. Bring friends and family to your celebration as a testimony of your faith in Jesus.

*Baptism is one way you share your new chapter
in life with the world.*

Look up the following scriptures. Pray and ask God for insight. Write in your journal or use the space provided to write what these scriptures mean to you.

Matthew 3:16

Matthew 28:19-20

Service

There are so many ways to serve God. I could write several books on this subject alone! Where do you begin? With a willing heart. Serving is a gift you give, but the blessing received is often flowing in both directions. You may be giving your time and talent to help someone in need, but God returns the blessing to you "pressed down, shaken together and running over" (Luke 6:38 NIV).

Identifying how God has gifted you or even what you enjoy doing may help you decide where you want to serve. The church I attend offers a class to help you identify your gifts and areas where you might choose to volunteer within the church or community. If you love children, you can serve in the children's department of your church or find a community group that allows volunteers in this area. If you love to sing or play an instrument you could considering trying out for the worship team. If you feel passionate about the elderly, you may visit an assisted living or nursing home, take meals to someone living alone, or even offer to do yard or housework for an elderly neighbor.

Serving is especially fun with a group. Maybe your city or church has a SERVE DAY where you can sign up online and serve with friends or your church small group. God equips you to serve in an area He has uniquely planned for you. As you humble yourself, God will direct you into the place you'll best benefit others and fulfill His plan for your life.

Look up the following scriptures. Pray and ask God for insight. Write in your journal or use the space provided to write what these scriptures mean to you.

Mark 10:45

Luke 6:38

Sharing your Story

Your story has purpose and will be one avenue God uses so others can see His love and transforming power. Your story of where you were before Christ came into your life, the steps you took to include God in your life, accepting Him, and what He is now doing in your life is all a part of His wonderful redemption story.

Telling your story can be done in many ways. Like me, you can meet up with people at a coffee shop and over time share bits and pieces of your story and what God has done for you. You can share in a small group or even just one-on-one with a friend or family member.

If God impresses on your heart, you may want to share in front of a larger group or write a book like me. God will prepare you and direct you to share your story as you grow in your relationship with Him. Before long your testimony will shine and be a light for others who want to know more about Jesus.

If you have any questions, feel free to reach out to our website at ohsofreeministries.com or OHSOFREE App. Hope to see you there!

Look up the following scriptures. Pray and ask God for insight. Write in your journal or use the space provided to write what these scriptures mean to you.

1 Peter 3:15

Acts 1:8

Dear Friend

It's my hope you've felt my love reaching out to you through this study. I hope you'll take steps to know more about God, have many intimate conversations with Him, and grow to be more like Him. The Apostle Paul prayed this prayer for the Ephesian Church. I pray this same prayer for you.

"When I think of all this, I fall to my knees and pray to the Father, the Creator of everything in heaven and on earth. I pray that from his glorious, unlimited resources he will empower you with inner strength through his Spirit. Then Christ will make his home in your hearts as you trust in him. Your roots will grow down into God's love and keep you strong. And may you have the power to understand, as all God's people should, how wide, how long, how high, and how deep his love is. May you experience the love of Christ, though it is too great to understand fully. Then you will be made complete with all the fullness of life and power that comes from God.

Now all glory to God, who is able, through his mighty power at work within us, to accomplish infinitely more than we might ask or think. Glory to him in the church and in Christ Jesus through all generations forever and ever! Amen." (Ephesians 3:14-21)

Acknowledgements

To Critique Girls #8: Thank you for the many hours of critiquing my *that's* and becoming my Writers Group girlfriends. You were there from the beginning of this journey and will continue to be my dear friends.

To Denise Michaels my Book and Marketing Coach: I'm so thrilled I found you. I'm amazed at your knowledge of the industry and how gifted you can speedily critique with excellence. Thank you for helping me with everything from the book to the ministry.

To Erin Suchy my Book Cover and Website Photographer: Coincidence? Absolutely, not! God connected us at just the right time. You are the easiest most gracious photographer I've ever worked with. You have a way of making everyone feel comfortable. You stopped being a stranger the minute you walked into the room. Now you are part of our family!

To Jaclyn Lepien: God used you to fine tune my direction. Your counsel to "ask God to prepare you for your future" helped me to take a big breath, exhale and step out into my calling. Thank you!

To Kathie Scriven my Content Editor: Thank you for your insightful suggestions on the manuscript, praying for me, and passing along so many great network opportunities.

To SHE Small Group: Thank you from the bottom of my heart. You were the first to hear my testimony. You offered love and grace while my voice was shaking. You've encouraged me consistently and kept me accountable in my relationship with Jesus. Thank you, girls. I love you!

To Terri Findley my Line Editor: God surprised me when you stepped back into my life and jumped outside the beta reader mold to become my line editor. For that, I'm thankful.

To Toni Chism and Author buddy: It wasn't just the coffee or that you too were on the same journey to be an Author as me. Our friendship has grown over the past year and I know God is going to continue to cross our paths. Thank you for all your powerful prayers!

To Vanessa Mendozzi my Cover and Formatting Designer: I'm so thankful I found you. You allowed me to relax and be at ease with the process because you're so talented and quick to answer my questions. I love my cover!

Connect with Darla

Website: www.ohsofreeministries.com

Email: ohsofree@protonmail.com

Helpful Resources

DENISE M. MICHAEL

Book Coach and Ghostwriter International
Writing Guild, Las Vegas, NV
www.ibwguild.com | fb/denise.michaels.585 | in/denisemm

ERIN SUCHY

erinsuchyphotography@gmail.com
www.erinsuchyphotography.mypixieset.com

KATHIE SCRIVEN

Scriven Communications Freelance Book Editor
kathiescriven@yahoo.com | fb/kathieneescriven

SAMANTHA DECKER

www.samanthadeckerwrites.com
www.redbudcontent.com

VANESSA MENDOZZI

www.vanessamendozzidesign.com

Resource Guide

Chapter 1

1. Chuck Sweeny: "The English language is doing fine, add a word if you like," https://www.journalstandard.com/news/20160824/chuck-sweeny-english-language-is-doing-fine-add-word-if-you-like
2. Lysa TerKeurst, "What Happens When Women Say Yes to God," (Oregon: Harvest House Publishers, 2007).

Chapter 2

3. Mark W. Baker, "How Embracing Vulnerability Can Change Your Spiritual Life," July 11, 2018 https://www.relevantmagazine.com.
4. Tracie Miles, "Get Real," posted by Proverbs 31 on October 12, 2007, (https://proverbs31.org/read/devotions/full-post/2007/10/12/get-real-4)

Chapter 3

5. Dr. David Ward, "Rejection Issues from Childhood to Now," https://www.m1psychology.com/rejection-issues-from-childhood-to-now/
6. Shannon Alder, https://theysaidso.com/quotes/author/shannon-l-alder

Chapter 4

7. Wendy Pope, "Hidden Potential," (Colorado:David C. Cook, 2020)

Chapter 6

8. Thomas Curran and Andrew P. Hill, "Perfectionism Is Increasing, and That's Not Good News," 2018, https://hbr.org/2018/01/perfectionism-is-increasing-and-thats-not-good-news

Chapter 7

9. Nancy DeMoss Wolgemuth, Article: 41 Evidences of Pride https://reviveourhearts.com | Fabienne Hartford, Article: "Seven Subtle Symptoms of Pride," https://www.desiringgod.org, July 15, 2015.

Chapter 10

10. Tim Keller, https://www.christianquotes.info/top-quotes/18-great-christian-quotes-about-marriage/.

Chapter 11

11. Tracy Dickens, https://instagram.com/sweetjoyfulsoul

www.ingramcontent.com/pod-product-compliance
Lightning Source LLC
Chambersburg PA
CBHW051241130726
47988CB00001B/450